Elements in the Politics of Development
edited by
Rachel Beatty Riedl
Einaudi Center for International Studies and Cornell University
Ben Ross Schneider
Massachusetts Institute of Technology
Maya Tudor
Oxford University

CONSTRUCTING ECONOMIC NATIONALISMS IN BRAZIL AND INDIA

Jason Jackson
Massachusetts Institute of Technology

Shaftesbury Road, Cambridge CB2 8EA, United Kingdom

One Liberty Plaza, 20th Floor, New York, NY 10006, USA

477 Williamstown Road, Port Melbourne, VIC 3207, Australia

314–321, 3rd Floor, Plot 3, Splendor Forum, Jasola District Centre, New Delhi – 110025, India

103 Penang Road, #05–06/07, Visioncrest Commercial, Singapore 238467

Cambridge University Press is part of Cambridge University Press & Assessment, a department of the University of Cambridge.

We share the University's mission to contribute to society through the pursuit of education, learning and research at the highest international levels of excellence.

www.cambridge.org
Information on this title: www.cambridge.org/9781009598576

DOI: 10.1017/9781009393607

© Jason Jackson 2026

This publication is in copyright. Subject to statutory exception and to the provisions of relevant collective licensing agreements, with the exception of the Creative Commons version the link for which is provided below, no reproduction of any part may take place without the written permission of Cambridge University Press & Assessment.

An online version of this work is published at doi.org/10.1017/9781009393607 under a Creative Commons Open Access license CC-BY-NC 4.0 which permits re-use, distribution and reproduction in any medium for non-commercial purposes providing appropriate credit to the original work is given and any changes made are indicated. To view a copy of this license visit https://creativecommons.org/licenses/by-nc/4.0

When citing this work, please include a reference to the DOI 10.1017/9781009393607

First published 2026

A catalogue record for this publication is available from the British Library

ISBN 978-1-009-59857-6 Hardback
ISBN 978-1-009-39361-4 Paperback
ISSN 2515-1584 (online)
ISSN 2515-1576 (print)

Cambridge University Press & Assessment has no responsibility for the persistence or accuracy of URLs for external or third-party internet websites referred to in this publication and does not guarantee that any content on such websites is, or will remain, accurate or appropriate.

For EU product safety concerns, contact us at Calle de José Abascal, 56, 1°, 28003 Madrid, Spain, or email eugpsr@cambridge.org

Constructing Economic Nationalisms in Brazil and India

Elements in the Politics of Development

DOI: 10.1017/9781009393607
First published online: January 2026

Jason Jackson
Massachusetts Institute of Technology
Author for correspondence: Jason Jackson, jbrj@mit.edu

Abstract: While the concept of economic nationalism is frequently deployed it is often poorly defined, posited as the cause of protectionism in some cases while providing a rationale for liberalization in others. This Element provides a more rigorous articulation by analyzing variation in foreign investment regulation in postwar Brazil and India. Conventional approaches cite India's leftist "socialism" and Brazil's right-wing authoritarianism to explain why India resisted foreign direct investment (FDI) while Brazil welcomed foreign firms. However, this ignores puzzling industry-level variation: India restricted FDI in auto manufacturing but allowed multinationals in oil, while Brazil welcomed foreign auto companies but prohibited FDI in oil. This variation is inadequately explained by pluralist theories, structural-material approaches, or constructivist ideas. This Element argues that FDI policies were shaped by contrasting colonial experiences that generated distinct economic nationalisms and patterns of industrialization in both countries. This title is also available as Open Access on Cambridge Core.

Keywords: Political Economy, International Development, Brazil, India, Foreign Investment

© Jason Jackson 2026

ISBNs: 9781009598576 (HB), 9781009393614 (PB), 9781009393607 (OC)
ISSNs: 2515-1584 (online), 2515-1576 (print)

Contents

1 Introduction — 1

2 Conceptualizing Economic Policy Preferences — 7

3 Reconsidering the Role of Economic Nationalism in Development — 20

4 Structural Similarities, Sociohistorical Differences: Brazil and India Compared — 30

5 Historicizing the Colonial Roots of Economic Nationalisms in Brazil and India — 38

6 The Development of the Oil Industry in Brazil and India — 48

7 The Development of the Auto Industry in India and Brazil — 62

8 Conclusion — 77

References — 82

1 Introduction

The global economy lay in ruins at the end of the Second World War. More than five years of conflict had decimated economies and societies across the world, whether through direct military bombardment or through pervasive shortages of key goods as international trade was severely disrupted in some places, and ground to a halt in others. With the end of the war, national and global efforts were redirected from waging war or simply surviving the conflict, to reconstruction and development. The challenges, while monumental, were similar across most spaces. Yet there was significant uncertainty about the optimal economic policy approach to chart a way forward, both to rebuild war-ravaged economies, particularly those at the center of the European and Asian war theatres, and to restructure newly emerging economies that were breaking free from colonial control and declaring independence as part of the decolonization wave that was sweeping across the world. The challenges facing developing countries were particularly compelling with the collective recognition that countries in the "periphery" faced a novel set of challenges with navigating a transformed geopolitical world order. Yet despite the commonalities in the economic policy problems that these countries faced, there were striking differences in the range of approaches that were adopted. Why was this so? Why do policymakers facing similar challenges make different economic policy choices?

Brazil and India Compared

Brazil and India serve as excellent cases for comparative analysis of the variation that arises in approaches to economic policy and development strategy. Postwar India and Brazil are both considered as epitomes of the statist developmentalist and nationalist economic policies that characterized much of the developing as well as advanced industrialized world in the wake of the Second World War (1945–1960). Both countries were intent on promoting rapid industrial development as a means of raising national incomes and establishing economic sovereignty in a neo-imperialist global political economy, and they also faced similar challenges with accessing finance and technology that were the keys to developing a modern industrial economy. As such, policymakers in both countries recognized that foreign direct investment (FDI) could play an important role in national development programs to promote economic growth and structural transformation. However, despite occupying similar structural positions in the global economy, facing similar material constraints, and being exposed to similar economic ideas and development strategies, India and Brazil pursued strikingly different approaches to regulating foreign investment. This variation is thus inadequately explained by conventional pluralist, structural-materialist, and even most constructivist approaches.

This Element analyzes this variation by comparing FDI policy approaches to sectoral development in natural resource extraction and manufacturing in both countries. India restricted FDI in manufacturing industries such as automobiles in order to facilitate the establishment of domestic business, but allowed multinationals corporations to establish dominant positions in natural resource-based sectors like petroleum. In contrast, Brazil welcomed foreign companies to launch its nascent automobile industry, but strongly prohibited FDI in oil. This was so even as policymakers in both countries were exposed to the same prevailing economic theories and policy ideas about how to promote industrial development and economic growth. This pattern of variation within and across both countries is summarized in Figure 1.[1] This Element thus addresses the following puzzle: Why did India and Brazil regulate FDI in such strikingly different ways?

This Element argues that Brazil and India developed distinct forms of economic nationalism. These were outcomes of social and political contestation arising from their contrasting colonial and early independence experiences. In Brazil, a "natural resource" form of economic nationalism emerged from a deep-seated belief in the existence of vast mineral riches, including oil, coupled with a powerful sense that neo-imperial forces were ruthlessly seeking to control them.[2] By contrast, in India a "manufacturing" form of economic

	OIL	AUTOS
BRAZIL	Restrictive	Liberal
INDIA	Liberal	Restrictive

Figure 1 Contrasting patterns of foreign direct investment policy in Brazil and India

---

[1] Please note that the typologies of "liberal" and "restricted" are not intended to suggest that industries were either completely open or closed to foreign capital, but rather to indicate the prevailing approach to regulating the participation of foreign firms. These distinctions are further elaborated through the case studies, for example, with an important metric being the relative degree of ownership and control by foreign and domestic actors.

[2] Resource nationalism is a familiar concept in international political economy, international management, and adjacent fields (see, for example, Click and Weiner, 2009, for a discussion). Yet despite a lineage dating as far back as the 1950s, it remains surprisingly underspecified (Ostrovski, 2023). This Element further develops this concept by grounding it in specific sets of anti-imperial beliefs and through comparison with the "manufacturing" variety of economic nationalism in the Indian case.

nationalism emerged from the belief that British colonialism *deindustrialized* India, derailing it from its natural path to industrial development. This was based on the idea that Indian artisans had world-renowned technical skills in areas such as textiles and dyes that were superior to those in the West well before the arrival of the British East India Company. In this view, it was the imposition of British "free trade" policies under colonial rule that destroyed these skills and stymied the development of Indian industry. These contrasting sources of nationalist beliefs had crucial importance for the regulation of key industries in the postwar period when the industrial foundation of both countries was being established. These are briefly previewed next and elaborated throughout the Element.

Automobiles

Brazil is well known to have actively encouraged foreign firm entry as a central part of its strategy to establish a motor vehicle industry. However, this approach involved suprisingly little effort to promote domestic firms as lead assemblers. Instead, multinational corporations were encouraged to establish dominant positions at the apex of the industry while Brazilian firms were incorporated in subordinate roles either as minority investment partners in assembly firms or as component suppliers, typically in minority joint ventures with foreign firms. By contrast, foreign firms were important participants in the nascent Indian automobile industry, but were not allowed to establish positions of managerial control. Even a major multinational firm like General Motors, which had been operating in India from as early as the 1920s, was forced to exit India after independence as private domestic firms such as Hindustan Motors, Tata Motors, and Premier Motors were promoted as vehicle assemblers and as component suppliers. Foreign firms were only allowed to be minority joint venture partners with private Indian firms.

Oil

Comparative analysis of the development of the petroleum sector reveals entirely different approaches to engaging with foreign capital. While the Brazilian state welcomed foreign firms into the automobile industry, multinationals were excluded from the petroleum sector, albeit after extensive political wrangling over foreign firms' role involving political elites, military officers, and societal groups, including labor and students. Instead, the state-owned Petrobrás was created with exclusive monopoly rights in exploration and refining, even though widely held optimism about the possible existence of large oil reserves was completely unfounded as there was no evidence of proven reserves at the time.

India took precisely the opposite approach. Conventional perspectives of India as a bastion of anti-foreign sentiment fail to explain why Prime Minister Jawaharlal Nehru's government allowed the overseas oil "majors" – widely considered to be the most nefarious of the multinationals – to occupy a lead role in exploration, refining, and distribution of its petroleum resources.[3] Further, India took this surprisingly liberal approach to the oil multinationals at the same time that it was touting its role as a leader among newly independent states asserting the right to economic sovereignty and self-determination in settings like the 1955 Asia-Africa Conference in Bandung. Even more surprising is that India took these steps in a moment when the oil majors were being chastened by waves of expropriation and nationalization in other developing countries.

Petroleum may seem like an unusual case through which to compare industrial development in Brazil and India. Today, Brazil is well known as a global petroleum producer, while India rarely figures in conversations about oil. Yet this is somewhat misleading. India is currently ranked 24th in global proven reserves, while Brazil is 15th. In fact, India has greater proven reserves than well-known oil producing nations such as Indonesia and Oman, and India's reserves are a more than half those of major global producers such as Mexico. Even more relevantly for this comparative study of the immediate postwar period, unlike Brazil, there was evidence that India might have oil reserves dating back to the nineteenth century and crucially, India had *higher* levels of proven oil reserves than Brazil for the first few decades of the postwar period. By contrast, Brazil's major petroleum discoveries are largely a late twentieth-century phenomenon. Why then would postwar India be more open to foreign investment in the oil sector than Brazil? And conversely, why was Brazil willing to cede control of the auto industry to foreign firms while India sought to establish its own national producers?

To make sense of this puzzle this Element traces the emergence of contrasting economic nationalisms in both countries from the late nineteenth century through the early postwar period. This approach centers the role of colonial experience in shaping economic nationalist beliefs and ensuing economic policy outcomes. It does so by developing an explanatory framework that avoids privileging culture over materiality by recognizing the duality of

---

[3] The oil majors comprised the so-called "seven sisters" that include Exxon, Mobil, and Chevron, the companies that emerged the Standard Oil Trust after was broken up by the US Supreme Court in 1911, as well as the US-based Gulf Oil and Texaco, British Petroleum (BP) and the Anglo-Dutch company Shell. After the Second World War, the Compagnie Française des Pétroles (later Total S.A.) was added to the seven sisters to form the group referred to as the oil majors (Ostrovski, 2023).

subjective-cultural and objective-material determinants of foreign investment policy preferences, as well as the role of societal contestation in shaping the emergence of distinct forms of economic nationalisms in India and Brazil.

Economic Nationalism

Many observers see the recent return of economic nationalism as a paradox of neoliberal globalization. While economic nationalism had long been recognized as a fundamental feature of the global economy, until recently it was considered an artifact of nineteenth-century imperial rivalries that led to twentieth-century wars. In this view, the final flickering flames of economic nationalism were extinguished as the anti-colonial euphoria of the postwar decolonization wave of the 1950s–1960s met the grim realities of the twin oil shocks in the 1970s. This marked the beginning of an era of economic crisis, structural adjustment, and globalization that constituted the neoliberal turn. Economic nationalism was thus consigned to the dustbin of history.

Yet, a few decades later, economic nationalism is once again recognized as a defining characteristic of the contemporary global political economy. Nationalist fervor is raging across large and small countries in both the developing and industrialized world. Contemporary economic nationalism has taken on several distinct forms, ranging from nativist and ethnocentric nationalism in diverse settings across Asia, Europe, Latin America, and the United States, to neo-mercantilist nationalisms driven by escalating geopolitical rivalries between emerging and declining global powers. Indeed, these forms of economic nationalism are not mutually exclusive. They combine different ideas, ideals, and beliefs, often creating novel – if seemingly convoluted and often contradictory – forms of economic nationalism.

Twenty-first-century economic nationalist fervor was initially activated by the global financial crisis of 2007–8, which was characterized by national-level responses to what was fundamentally a crisis of the deeply interconnected global economy. Nationalist ferment grew through the 2010s with growing reactions to deeper structural features of the globalized world economy that was constructed in the 1980s and 1990s through neoliberal international trade and investment policies. These tensions reached crisis points with the sudden disruption created by the COVID-19 pandemic and deep societal inequalities that the pandemic laid bare, and persist with the growing range of social, political, and economic tensions and conflicts that are manifesting across the globe due to the climate crisis. Finally, all these have been exacerbated by the rise and pervasive use of digital technologies, which have created spaces for nationalist sentiment to grow, seemingly unchecked, as efforts to moderate online discourse are diluted or outright abandoned.

These developments have had concrete impacts on economic policymaking, making clear the need to understand contemporary economic nationalism in all its various manifestations. But our conceptual and analytic tools are not adequate for the task. Existing theories of economic nationalism provide oversimplified analyses that risk producing misleading conclusions about the role of nationalist beliefs in the economic policymaking process. This Element offers a different approach.

Chapter Organization

The rest of this Element is organized as follows. Section 2 offers a rigorous treatment of the relationship between economic interests and policy preferences, highlighting the strengths and limitations of currently dominant approaches. Section 3 builds on this foundation with a reconsideration of economic nationalism as a concept and a discussion of how the interdisciplinary scholarship on economic nationalism has evolved. A key element of economic nationalism is, of course, how nationalist beliefs are translated into economic policy preferences. With this foundation in theories of economic nationalism and policy preferences in place, Section 4 discusses the rationale for the case selection and the comparative approach that is adopted, highlighting the advantages of leveraging the Brazilian and Indian cases in the study of economic nationalism. The Element then turns to the sources of differing economic nationalisms in Brazil and India and the implications for the regulation of foreign direct investment and multinational firms in Section 5. It does so by providing a historical analysis of the origins and evolution of contrasting economic nationalisms in Brazil and India, highlighting the role of colonial experience in shaping different nationalist beliefs in both countries. This provides the foundation for the contrasting cases of the development of the oil and automobile industries in both countries, which are presented in Sections 6 and 7 respectively. The analysis in these two sections utilizes primary archival materials, particularly from diplomatic communiques between American consular and embassy officials in Brazil and India and their counterparts in the State Department in Washington DC. Consular officials played key roles in observing and assessing the investment climate in the countries where they were stationed, submitting frequent commentaries and reports and often serving as intermediaries between American businesses and local companies and government officials. As such, these documents provide a rich insight into the views of Indian policy and business elites, as well as the perspectives of American multinational firms that were considering investing in those countries or had active operations. Section 8 provides conclusions, including brief consideration of why economic nationalism leads to statist ownership in some country-industry cases, and private control in others using the example of the formation of the steel industry in both countries. It discusses some of the implications for understanding the role of economic nationalism in contemporary global developments and identifies important areas for future research.

2 Conceptualizing Economic Policy Preferences

Political science still asks all too rarely why an actor believed the means he adopted would have the effects he anticipated and where those beliefs originated. When we say that an actor, whether an individual or a government, took a particular set of actions to further his interests, even if we know what his interests were, we need to know why he had any reason to believe such actions would serve those interests well.[4]

Preferences, interests, and ideas are key analytic concepts used to explain economic policy decisions and outcomes in comparative and international political economy and the political economy of development. This is especially so in the "new" institutionalisms, whether the rational choice, historical institutional, or sociological variants that simultaneously re-emerged as distinct paradigms in the 1980s and 1990s (Hall and Taylor, 1996). This renewed interest in the study of institutions – defined as rules and norms that shape social and individual behavior – has produced an increasingly fruitful interdisciplinary exchange in the social sciences.[5] This recognition revealed commonalities among the competing paradigmatic approaches to institutions that in turn has led to growing theoretical dialogue (Immergut, 1998; Thelen, 1999; Campbell and Pederson, 2001; North, 2005; Katznelson and Weingast, 2005; Scott, 2008; Hall, 2010). It has also become increasingly apparent in empirical work (Mahoney, 2000; Acemoglu and Robinson, 2005; Greif, 2006; Mahoney and Thelen, 2010).[6]

The literature sees preferences, interests, institutions, and ideas playing an important role in shaping human action. Yet competing paradigms disagree on

---

[4] Hall (2005: 135).
[5] This is particularly so as scholars realized that the debate about institutions over the past three decades was due less to paradigmatic wars than to each approach responding to the behaviorism of the 1960s (Hall and Taylor, 1996; Immergut, 1998). The behaviorist approach sought to apply "scientific" methods to human behavior through a focus on the individual at the expense of institutions, as well as an emphasis on deductive rather than interpretive approaches.
[6] In addition to theoretical arbitrage, this has also been reflected in methodological innovation, where the analytic methods that have traditionally been associated with particularly approaches – statistical analysis and game theory in rational choice, archival research and macro-historical narrative in historical institutionalism, and ethnographic and other interpretive methods in sociological institutionalism—are now being employed to a greater degree across approaches, as evinced in the trend toward multi-method research.

the constitution of actors, interests, and institutions, and the nature and direction of the causal relationship between them. This reveals a twin tension in what Immergut (1998) referred to as the "theoretical core" of the new institutionalisms. There is a tension between materialist and constructivist sources of preferences and interests, and a tension between structure and agency. The location of different institutional approaches on each of these intersecting dimensions provides distinct theoretical predictions of the sources of interests and preferences that shape economic agents' political behavior and produces policy and economic outcomes.

This Element focuses on the role of nationalist beliefs in shaping the institutions governing foreign direct investment (FDI) policy in postwar Brazil and India. Institutions and ideas play an important role in shaping actors' FDI policy preferences by ascribing different roles to foreign and domestic firms in the Brazilian and Indian economies. But institutions themselves are created through dynamic and contested sociopolitical processes as actors struggle to shape the rules, norms, and beliefs that govern economic life.

Analyzing the role of economic nationalism in FDI policy reveals how competing theories predicting that economic and political actors' policy preferences are naturally endowed, are determined by socioeconomic structural position, or are produced by rational calculation are misleading. Preferences toward FDI are neither fixed nor structurally determined; they are malleable and are created through ideas and beliefs that emerge from historical processes of social construction and political contestation.

Theorizing Preferences and Interests in Political Economy

Economic interests and policy preferences are fundamental conceptual building blocks in political economic analysis of the policymaking process. Preferences are central to accounts of purposive action, but leading scholars from different analytic traditions nevertheless lament that "preferences remain a relatively primitive category of analysis" (Katznelson and Weingast, 2005). The challenges appear to be fundamental: "scholarly attention to the sources of national or sub-national interests – or, as we call them, preferences – is wrought with confusion" (Frieden, 1999: 39).[7] As such, it is critical to establish clear definitions of interests and preferences as distinct, though related, concepts at the outset of this analysis of economic nationalism and foreign investment policy.

---

[7] In later work, Frieden and Lake (2005: 149) provide a clarified distinction in which interests are defined as how individuals or groups are affected by particular policies, with preferences relating to different policy options. This is closer to the definition that I provide next.

In his rich intellectual history, *The Passions and the Interests*, Hirschman (1977) interrogates the rise of material interests as a historically specific political construct. The concept of "interests" served to facilitate the capitalist transition by taming the destructive "passions" of the sovereigns and promoting their "interests" in material gains through peaceful commerce. Hirschman defines interests as "valued ends." Interests reflect the ultimate outcomes or states of being that economic actors want to achieve. Preferences and interests are intimately related: Preferences refer to economic actors' conceptions of available alternatives that they believe will allow them to achieve their desired ends.[8] Ideas and beliefs about means–ends relationships, such as those positing a linkage between foreign investment policies and development outcomes, are thus central to the substantive content of policy preferences.

This content is provided by economic theories that posit causal relationships between FDI and development outcomes.[9] However, there are competing theories and ideas at play in the scholarly and policy literature on the developmental role of FDI. This reflects a crucial ambiguity that has long been at the heart of FDI policy conflicts: is foreign capital good or bad for development? This ambiguity creates space for political contestation between economic and political actors wielding competing ideas as they battle to shape the policy and institutional environment in their favor (Beland and Cox, 2011). The process through which actors acquire those beliefs underpins the always-contested sociopolitical dynamics of preference formation (Hall, 2005: 155).[10]

---

[8] The corollary in the microfoundations of neoclassical economic theory would be utility, which is a measure of satisfaction and is synonymous with interests. Preferences would reflect the bundle of goods that an actor believes would maximize her utility, i.e. allow her to achieve her interests. See also North's (2005: 23) discussion of the role of beliefs in determining choices, which in turn shape social structure. Belief formation – and the cognitive processes of learning that underpin them – is central in his theory of institutional change. Elster (2005: 248) defines preferences as "a preference ordering over policy options." Further, "An outcome-oriented motivation needs to be supplemented with causal beliefs to yield a policy preference. More simply: to achieve an end you need to form a belief about means to that end. This is true of the pursuit of common interest as well as of private interest."

[9] This emphasis on the content of policy preferences is consistent with calls from scholars of economic nationalism to focus on the nature of nationalist content (Abdelal, 2001; Helleiner, 2002). Economic ideas and nationalist beliefs combine to shape preferences, as this section and the empirical analysis that follows will show.

[10] As such, this Element considers the preferences of both business and state actors in understanding the effects of economic nationalism on FDI policy outcomes in Brazil and India. The former are important as key participants (along with other societal groups) in the process of policy contestation, while the latter are the ultimate decision-makers.

Structural Weaknesses: Deducing Policy Preferences from Structural Position

The conventional approach to determining policy preferences in comparative and international political economy – whether its rational choice or historical institutional variants – is to derive economic actors' policy preferences from their structural position.

The widely held proposition that domestic incumbent firm preferences will lead them to lobby against FDI liberalization draws support from neoclassical economics. Neoclassical theory predicts that "supernormal" monopoly profits come from imperfectly competitive industries (Tirole, 1988). This provides incumbent producers in profitable concentrated industries with an incentive to prevent entry of competitors to protect their monopoly profits (Stigler, 1971). Private interests are thus expected to organize and lobby for the private non-welfare maximizing benefits of protection (Olson, 1965; Stigler, 1971; Peltzman, 1976; Grossman and Helpman, 1994).

In this view, multinational corporations (MNCs) pose a serious competitive threat to domestic incumbents, particularly those located in developing countries. MNCs are conceptualized as an organizational manifestation of transnational capital that is seeking higher returns on firm-specific assets, that is, resources that a given firm owns or controls, including physical assets such as land, machinery, and buildings as well as intangible assets such as knowledge, technologies, capabilities, and organizational routines and practices. While international portfolio capital expects to capture returns via the theory of factor price equalization (the process by which the prices of factors of production are expected to equalize across countries through international trade), owners of firm-specific capital are vulnerable to incomplete contracting problems (where contracts between firms may not account for all possible contingencies) and thus avoid arms-length market transactions. Establishing a physical presence in foreign markets through FDI is an organizational solution to securing returns on firm-specific assets such as proprietary technology, production capabilities, or brand name. Multinational firms thus set up operations in foreign countries and "go it alone."

Once established in a new country context, particularly when characterized by an underdeveloped industrial sector such as in most newly independent countries, multinationals can have major disruptive effects on the existing market structure. The question is, will those disruptive effects be net negative or positive? And how will the gains and losses be distributed between foreign and domestic capital, and other societal groups such as labor and the communities in which the firms operate? Scholars of international business have tended to address these distributional questions through analysis of structural dynamics. MNCs tend to operate in oligopolistic industries, where a few firms produce the majority of output and capture most of the market (Caves, 1996). Their deep pockets and superior access to technology allow them to overcome foreign market entry barriers and the "liability of foreignness" or disadvantages that arise from their unfamiliarity with the cultural, political, and economic features of the local environment as well as their outsider status (Zaheer, 1995). However, once established, MNCs' firm-specific resources and capabilities are translated into competitive advantages that threaten to reduce domestic incumbents' income and market share, increase competition in labor and product markets, and pressure domestic incumbents to exit (Barney, 1991; Caves, 1996).[11]

Once again, this raises the issue of power relations between foreign and domestic firms. Yet the role of geopolitics, states, and economic nationalism is strikingly absent in this rational characterization of the behavior of multinational capital, a point to which this Element will return. Instead, dominant analytic approaches for determining domestic firms' policy preferences in the rational-materialist tradition have largely relied on deduction from theoretical expectations of changes in firm income and profits arising from the implementation of alternative policy options. The main divide, broadly applied in the politics of international economic relations, is between factor-and sector-based approaches in neoclassic trade theory. Factor-based approaches rely on the assumptions of the Stolper-Samuelson (1941) theorem, which suggests that when factors of production can move freely between sectors, policy shifts from protection to liberalization will increase the income of owners of factors that are relatively abundant in the economy (i.e. those in which the economy is well endowed) and lower the income of owners of the relative scarce factors (i.e. those in which the economy is poorly endowed). In developing country contexts like postwar India and Brazil, owners and intensive users of scarce factors (usually capital) will be expected to support protection while owners and intensive users of abundant factors (usually labor) will be expected to support liberalization. Policy conflicts are expected to emerge from differences in preferences between broad class coalitions, which in turn are based on a given country's factor endowments (cf. Rogowski, 1989; Scheve and Slaughter, 1998).

---

[11] The alternative argument in the economics and international business literatures holds that FDI may benefit domestic firms through productivity-improving technology spillovers, but this is largely absent from the international political economy literature on the politics of FDI (though see Pandya, 2014). However, this plays an important part in the actual politics of FDI policy, as I show later in this Element.

By contrast, sector-based approaches rely on the Ricardo-Viner model. It assumes that at least one factor is fixed such that factors associated with sectors facing foreign competition lose from liberalization. Following this model, and to the extent they are immobile, both capital and labor in import-substituting manufacturing sectors will be expected to oppose liberalization. Thus, as an example, capital and labor in the protected postwar Indian or Brazilian automobile industries should *both* oppose FDI reforms. Political conflicts are expected to occur across sectors with cross-class coalitions of capital, labor, and landowners who stand to benefit from liberalization on one side, pitted against cross-class coalitions that stand to lose on the other. The key is factor specificity, that is, the extent to which factors are closely tied to their sectors (cf. Milner, 1988).

In summary, both theories predict – albeit via different mechanisms – that industrial capital in developing countries such as India will resist liberalization and lobby for protection. How then can we explain similarly situated Indian and Brazilian government and firm actors' contrasting preferences for FDI in the immediate postwar period, when Indian automobile firms sought limitations on foreign capital participation in India while their Brazilian counterparts were far more welcoming to multinationals? Not only do both these structural-material frameworks fail to explain this sort of cross-national variation, these static approaches face challenges in explaining preference change, such as many Indian manufacturers' growing preferences for FDI reforms in the post-1991 liberalization era, which contrasted with greater resistance to foreign capital entry during the import substitution era. As Mark Blyth (2003) pithily noted, "structures do not come with an instruction sheet."

Open-economy Politics

The exclusive focus on material sources of preferences in the literature merits further attention. In many respects, Peter Gourevitch's (1986) claim that "what people want depends on where they sit" might be seen as the early forerunner of material interest-based approaches in comparative and international political economy (Blyth, 2009). However, the analytic move to combine political analysis with economic theory as described in the previous section aimed to provide parsimony and predictive power, albeit at the cost of Gourevitch's richness (Blyth, 2009). David Lake argues that deducing interests is the essential innovation of "open economy politics," which "begins with sets of individuals – firms, sectors, factors of production – that can reasonably be assumed to share (nearly) identical interests" and derives preferences over economic policy from each actor's structural location (Lake, 2009: 50). Indian firms' FDI policy preferences would thus be deduced from their structural position relative to multinational competitors in the global economy. These assumptions are vigorously defended as the standard for comparative and international political economy (Frieden and Martin, 2002; Lake, 2009).

The conundrum of economic nationalism lies at the core of these approaches. It led to the development of the open economy politics (OEP) approach in the 1970s, which sought to explain the significant variation in protectionism that was observed across countries and industries, and over time. It was rooted in dissatisfaction with earlier political economic analyses that were seen as unsystematic and lacking rigor. By contrast, the adoption of deductive economic approaches such as those based on "rigorous" Ricardo-Viner and Stolper-Samuelson trade theories produced testable hypotheses and generalizable results thus underpinning a revolution in approaches to determining economic interests, policy preferences, and political economic outcomes (cf. Alt and Gilligan, 1994). Concrete materialist interests displaced what were seen to be fuzzy cultural and ideational objectives and motivations, particularly those characterized as economic nationalism.

While this analytic approach grew out of trade analyses such as Rogowski's (1989) well-known study of the sources of cleavages in political coalitions, it has been widely applied as the standard approach to non-trade areas of international economic relations, including international financial and monetary policy (Frieden, 1991, 1994, 2006), product markets (Keohane and Milner, 1996; Bates, 1998), labor markets (Rodrik, 1997; Iverson, 2005), and foreign direct investment (Pinto, 2003). Theoretical and empirical developments in OEP later led scholars to incorporate the impact of domestic and international political institutions as mechanisms of preference aggregation and sites of bargaining among competing societal interests at the domestic and interstate levels (Lake and Powell, 1999; Milner, 1999; Frieden and Lake, 2005).[12]

Once again, the enigma of economic nationalism served as a motivating force. Much of this research was conducted by economists and was driven by a normative question that puzzled many of its proponents who wondered, "Given that freer markets and economic liberalization is clearly good for countries, 'Why don't governments do what is *obviously* best for their societies?'" (Rodrik, 2008). By contrast, political scientists saw "protection as the norm" and sought to explain why countries would liberalize at all: "Politically, protection seem[ed] eminently reasonable" (Milner, 1999).

In economics, this question became a topic of interest for the voluminous public choice literature that applied neoclassical market analytic tools to non-market

---

[12] Frieden and Lake (2005) see work on the mutual interaction between domestic and international political economy that incorporates both levels of analysis without imposing artificial barriers between them as the next step in the OEP research program.

domains of social and political life. The mood of the time is best summarized by Gary Becker's pronouncement that "the [neoclassical] economic approach is a comprehensive one that is applicable to all human behavior" (Becker, 1976: 8). Economic policies were the outcome of the political influence of powerful rent-seeking interest groups rather than idiosyncratic nationalism (Buchanan and Tullock, 1962; Stigler, 1971; Buchanan, Tollison and Tullock, 1980; Grossman and Helpman, 1994).[13] Policy arenas characterized by diffuse costs and concentrated benefits such as trade and FDI were seen as particularly vulnerable to the rent-seeking activities of well-organized groups. Despite important criticisms, especially of the strict behavioral assumptions upon which it rested, the literature served to orient theorists to the distributional effects of economic policy and the implications for political action. We now turn to consider these three issues – behavioral assumptions, distribution considerations, and sociopolitical outcomes – in greater detail.

Preference Ambiguity

The core of the debate is about the nature and source of economic policy preferences. Structural deductive theories, either separately or in combination (e.g. Hiscox, 2002), have done much to advance scholarly understanding of the sources of economic policy preferences in comparative and international political economy. Nevertheless, they have important limitations. Deduced preferences do not explain what in reality are far more ambiguous responses to liberalization (Helleiner, 2002; Helleiner and Pickel, 2005). Economic actors reveal complex preferences that are a priori difficult to ascertain, even within a particular social class (e.g. capital or labor), sector (e.g. manufacturing or services), or industry (e.g. automobiles or pharmaceuticals). This has been demonstrated by empirical studies across a variety of country contexts (Schneider, 2004). Kingstone (1999) reveals how, contrary to expectations, Brazilian industrialists did not resist external liberalization in the late 1980s and 1990s. Segments of domestic capital that had earlier opposed liberalization changed positions and joined reformist politicians in a powerful coalition for free trade, despite decades of privileges under import substitution policies. Similarly, in Mexico, large domestic firms played a crucial role in supporting

---

[13] These developments in the subfield of political economy reflected the growing dominance of neoclassical theory in economics and its influence on other social science disciplines. Research programs in the political economy of development were significantly shaped by this public choice literature, particularly Krueger's seminal (1974) paper on the "political economy of the rent seeking society" as well as Bhagwati's (1982) formulation of "directly unproductive profit-seeking activities" (DUPs). See Maxfield and Schneider (1997) for a critique and discussion of how business collective action in developing countries can generate positive development outcomes.

Mexico's trade reforms in the late 1980s and early 1990s (Thacker, 2000). In both cases, entrenched domestic incumbents that had reaped significant gains from protection appeared to act against their structurally determined preferences, resulting in quite varied approaches to market liberalization.

Preference ambiguity is not limited to developing country contexts. Woll (2008) shows how major US and European telecommunications firms like AT&T, Deutsche Telekom, and France Telecom were uncertain of their policy positions over liberalization of the global telecommunications industry. She details how their preferences evolved over the course of the negotiations from resistance to active support. The same findings hold when examining firm preferences in other realms of business politics. Martin (1995, 2006) reveals the striking indeterminacy of US firms' preferences for healthcare and labor market policies in the 1990s and 2000s. She is joined by Swenson (1991) and Mares (2003) in a now well-established critique of approaches that read business preferences off structural capital-labor cleavages, instead showing how capital has in many cases pushed for pro-labor policies.

This Element builds on these scholars' work by pushing the critique of structural determinants of policy preferences one step further through the cases of Brazil and India. It shows how radically different preferences emerged from historically rooted variation in beliefs about the role of foreign versus domestic firms in the industrial development process and wider modernization project. These beliefs informed the development of distinct ideas linking FDI with industrial development outcomes. These economic ideas were underpinned by historical experiences that ascribed salient social meanings to the role of foreign capital in the pursuit of industrial modernity. Brazilian business and government actors welcomed multinational corporations as collaborative partners who could play a central role in capital accumulation and industrialization in the manufacturing sector. Their Indian counterparts also recognized that foreign firms were crucial sources of technology, but viewed them as potential neo-imperialist instruments, and hence were much more wary of engaging with multinationals.

Foreign capital was thus placed in contrasting categories in both countries. These policy positions were reversed when dealing with oil. The role of foreign capital was thus interpreted in different ways across industries in both countries. The upcoming sections provide empirical support for the view that economic actors' policy preferences cannot be deduced based on assumptions of material interests and structural position. Preferences are shaped by economic ideas that are imbued with historically salient social and political meaning. In the Brazilian and Indian cases these arise from colonial experiences that shape nationalist beliefs. Economic interests and policy preferences are not automatically given; preferences are formed through historically embedded sociopolitical processes that shape the experiences and beliefs of economic and political actors.

The Substantive Content of Policy Preferences: Role of Economic Ideas and Economic Nationalist Beliefs

The previous section argued that ideas drawn from economic theory are essential constitutive elements of economic policy preferences. Economic ideas provide the causal connection between a given policy and its economic outcomes and distributional effects. Hall (2005: 141) argues that these theories are "indispensable in the economic sphere since we do not see the economy with the naked eye but live in the imagined economies constructed by economic theory." Preferences thus turn heavily on the cause-effect relationships that are posited in prevailing economic theories (ibid.). This is reflected in the twentieth-century historical movement between theoretical paradigms of Keynesianism and Monetarism in the advanced industrialized countries, as well as from import substituting industrialization to economic liberalization in the developing world. These epochal movements between techno-economic institutional arrangements reflected shifts in distinct belief-systems based on competing economic technologies. The rise and fall of Keynesianism in the United States and Western Europe was the outcome of changing policy preferences (Blyth, 2002). So too were European governments' decisions to enter into monetary union (Hall, 2005). As was many developing countries' adoption of trade and investment policy packages associated with neoliberal globalization and the Washington Consensus. Further, governments are not alone in being susceptible to the ideas that drive these types of macro-institutional shifts; they also occur at the firm level as studies by Fligstein (1990) and Dobbin and Zorn (2005) on shifting logics of corporate governance showed, and to which the findings of this Element attest.

These theories are not simply technical artifacts, but rather function as mechanisms of distribution, power, and control. Just as the shift from Keynesianism to Monetarism is seen as having momentous distributional effects between capital and labor – by weakening labor union power, increasing inequality, and undermining the welfare state – so too have the predictions from economic theory about the effects of FDI policy provided the rationale for economic agents' belief that a liberal FDI policy regime will be either good or bad for a given sector, industry, or firm. These theories and the policies they imply directly determine distributional outcomes between foreign and domestic firms in Brazil and India. Preference formation is an inherently contentious and political process: it is a high-stakes game. However, the central role of economic theory in preference formation introduces an element of indeterminacy as economic theory itself often provides ambiguous policy direction to economic agents, particularly under conditions of uncertainty. This provides opportunities for economic agents to persuade others to pursue the courses of action that they believe will best allow them to achieve their interests. It also provides an explanation for why we see radically different policy approaches that are nevertheless underpinned by economic nationalist beliefs, whether in the postwar period, as I will show through the cases of Brazil and India, or in the period of neoliberalism and globalization as Helleiner (2002), Pickel (2021), and others have argued.

The indeterminacy of economic theory is well recognized in empirical studies of policymaking. Hall (2005) showed how after fifteen years of debate British officials were unsure of whether joining the European Monetary Union would advance the nation's interests. Even after inception the effects remained unclear. Certainly, in the context of FDI theory the relationship between FDI liberalization and economic outcomes for domestic firms has long been ambiguous. FDI liberalization may either lead to displacement of local companies as more efficient MNCs enter the market, or it may lead to increases in domestic firm productivity and market competitiveness through technological spillovers. These are the competing theories that shape FDI policy preferences and contestation between actors in the policy arena.

As previously discussed, arguments against FDI liberalization rest on the expected distributional effects of FDI reforms, where efficient MNCs threaten to outcompete and ultimately displace their inefficient domestic counterparts. By contrast, the main argument in favor of liberalizing FDI in a developing country context sees MNCs' superior technology as a potential advantage, suggesting that FDI facilitates productivity spillovers that domestic firms can capture. A brief review of the literature serves to highlight this issue. In early scholarship on FDI, Caves (1974) used sector-specific data to find positive productivity spillovers from MNCs to local firms. FDI was held to provide benefits through three distinct mechanisms: allocative efficiency through pro-competitive effects, technical efficiency through demonstration effects, and technology transfer by providing access to know-how on favorable terms (Caves, 1974). These and similar pro-FDI mechanisms were heavily promoted by powerful global actors such as the International Monetary Fund (IMF) and the World Bank as they pushed developing countries to adopt neoliberal economic reforms, including deregulated FDI regimes, from the 1980s onward.

These policies were promoted despite increasingly ambiguous evidence of the beneficial effects of FDI, even within mainstream economics. Aitken and Harrison (1999) critique studies using sectoral data by pointing to an identification problem: Studies focus on industries where domestic total factor productivity (TFP) is already high. They use Venezuelan plant-level panel data and a fixed effects model to show that FDI does not generate significant intra-industry productivity spillovers. Other studies have increasingly found negative effects across factor and product markets. Aitken, Harrison, and Lipsey (1996) found that domestic TFP was negatively impacted as foreign competitors bid up wages and hired away talented workers. Markussen and Venables (1999) found that local firm sales were hurt by MNC entry leading to productivity decreases from the effects of adjustment costs on input usage or the ability to capture scale economies. Later studies only increased the ambiguity by identifying contingent effects: Javorcik (2004) found vertical spillovers arising from backward linkages from MNC customers to their local suppliers, but no intra-industry effects through horizontal spillovers or forward linkages. Buckley et al. (2007) illustrated a potential temporal effect through an inverted U-shaped relationship, with TFP rising with small levels of MNC entry and then falling as more MNCs enter the market.[14] Finally, in addition to these findings by mainstream international economists that cast doubt on the benefits of FDI, heterodox development economists like Alice Amsden (2001, 2009) strenuously argued that multinational corporations pose a significant threat to domestic firms, crowding them out of the types of underdeveloped or "imperfect" markets that characterized developing economies.

This theoretical and empirical ambiguity in the scholarly literature raised serious questions about the actual economic effects of foreign investment, yet this uncertainty and ambiguity hardly deters economic agents from drawing on these arguments in their efforts to convince others of their preferred FDI strategy. On the contrary, these opposing economic arguments constitute valuable resources that are used by competing actors in their efforts to shape FDI rules to their liking, as the upcoming discussions of the Brazilian and Indian industry cases show. Ambiguity creates a space for politics that would likely be foreclosed if causal economic relationships were unquestioned. This policy contest to influence preferences and outcomes takes place in a variety of public

---

[14] From a political economy standpoint, it is important to note that most of these studies focus on the sectoral or industry level and say little about distribution among domestic firms. That is, even if there are positive spillover effects in a given industry such as autos or pharmaceuticals, *which* domestic firms might actually capture them? This ambiguity brings us back to the original critique of rational-material behavioral predictions arising from dominant political economy theories. It highlights the importance of uncertainty as well as heterogeneity in beliefs between actors in providing a role for politics and persuasion.

and private spaces. The domain of public discourse through the media has been an especially brutal battleground alongside closed-door discussions between individual firms, industry associations, lobbyists, and different representatives of the government. Domestic firms that believe they can benefit from technology transfer from MNCs push for joint venture rules that mandate local-foreign firm partnerships through joint ventures or local content requirements that stipulate the use of domestic suppliers. Other domestic firms that are skeptical of MNCs' positive impact on local players utilize theoretical arguments of market stealing effects to make their case. Foreign firms are also important players in this arena. They deploy theories purporting that FDI provides broad efficiency gains at the industry level and has implications for employment and economic growth that shape key actors' preferences and wider public opinion. In the absence of a scholarly and policy consensus, the legitimacy of these competing theoretical arguments relies on factors that are beyond the merits of the causal ideas themselves, including the social, economic, and political resources – which is to say the power – of economic agents striving to shape the field of FDI policy (Fligstein, 2008).[15] It also heavily relies on the extent to which competing actors are able to imbue these causal ideas with historically salient social meaning, such as compelling nationalist narratives, symbols, and tropes (Jackson, 2025).

Nationalist Narratives: Historical Salience and Social Meaning

Salient and socially meaningful symbols and narratives play a key role in shaping economic actors' policy preferences. Narratives are socially embedded cultural devices. They allow economic actors to make sense of the economic world by providing intersubjectively held interpretations of important events. These interpretations imbue the abstract causal relationships provided by economic theory with social meaning. Economic development and modernization can be viewed as a series of "societal projects" (Dobbin, 2004) that are based on a specific set of ideas – economic growth, industrialization, democracy – which are operationalized in the policy realm by following the prescriptions of prevailing social and economic theories that spell out the means to achieve them. In this respect "policy is only partly driven by material forces ... Its route also depends on sequence of events a nation faces and grand narratives devised to explain what it should do in the face of such events" (Hall, 2005: 137). History and the interpretation and social meaning of past events are thus central in understanding the policy preferences that actors hold.

---

[15] Social resources include legitimacy, economic resources capture the financial power that actors have to promote their preferred view, while political resources include personal relationships and connections with politicians, bureaucrats, and other key decision-makers.

Economic theory, nationalist narratives, and cultural symbols thus play mutually reinforcing roles in policymaking processes. Actors try to comprehend otherwise technical and ethereal economic policies by linking them to a larger sense of nation and history (Abdelal, 2001). As I have argued elsewhere, how else to make sense of the murky modalities of technological learning and the confusing prescriptions of contradictory economic theories than to connect it with stories of travail and triumph of entrepreneurial domestic firms? (Jackson, 2025: 25) Tata Steel's late nineteenth-century struggle to establish a domestic steel industry against strident foreign opposition before eventually prevailing against both the colonial government and British competitors and rescuing India's nascent railroad construction projects during the steel shortages of the First World War provides an excellent example. A century later at the beginning of the new millennium, popular conceptions of "new economy" IT giant Infosys redefined how India was viewed in the global economy and, even more importantly, how Indian firms were viewed at home (ibid.).

Analyzing how narratives are interpreted and reinterpreted over time provides insights to the contested nature of history. It allows for "discerning how one account comes to be accepted as 'what really happened' while other plausible stories are rejected" and provides a perspective from the worldview of actors of why, in a given context, certain actions are taken while others are either rejected or not considered at all (Ross, 2009: 149). Narratives are infused with symbols and metaphors that capture the imagination, galvanize potentially fractious groups, and motivate action; they imbue actors with "social purpose" (Abdelal, 2001). And just as economic theories are not mere technical artifacts, symbols, and narratives are not just stories. They are resources to be utilized by economic agents seeking to convey a particular understanding of the world and courses of actions that should be pursued.

We now turn to deeper consideration of the role of economic nationalism in industrial policy and economic development.

3 Reconsidering the Role of Economic Nationalism in Development

> " ... [we are witnessing] the re-emergence of a spectre from the darkest period of modern history ... Economic nationalism .... If it is not buried again forthwith, the consequences will be dire."
>
> – *The Economist*[16]

Theories of economic nationalism are a mainstay of comparative and international political economy, historical sociology, and international management

---

[16] *The Economist* 2009. "The Return of Economic Nationalism." February 5, 2009.

(Hymer, 1960; Abdelal, 2001; Gilpin, 2001; Helleiner, 2002; Helleiner and Pickel, 2005; Bonikowski, 2016). However, while economic nationalism is regularly deployed to explain external economic policies by academics, policy analysts, and the media, with few exceptions it is often ambiguously conceptualized and in the worst instances, such as *The Economist* quote earlier, merely serves as shorthand for protectionism. Even among leading scholars in the field, conceptions of economic nationalism have teetered between fuzzy perspectives of economic policymaking as emotional and irrational, to perspectives of economic nationalism as reflecting the rational pursuit of material interests. Economic historian Charles Kindleberger provided an excellent articulation of the latter view in describing policymakers as rationally responding to opposition to FDI arising from the "peasant, the populist, the mercantilist, or the nationalist which each of us harbors in his breast" by instituting protectionist economic policies that benefit domestic interests.[17] By contrast, economist Harry Johnson, a leading contributor to the growing field of international economics in the postwar period, "famously [and dismissively] ascribed many countries' protectionism to a 'taste for nationalism,' [and] a willingness to 'direct economic policy toward the production of psychic income in the form of nationalistic satisfaction, at the expense of material income'."[18]

These contradictory perspectives on economic nationalism are clearly unsatisfactory. While the conceptualization of economic nationalism has been sharpened over time, economic nationalism is still often posited as either romantically emotional or ideological, as with the Johnson quote, or are materialistic and hyperrational, as with Kindleberger's contribution. As noted in the previous section, competing theories of economic nationalism have benefited from developments in rational-deductive political economy as well as from the interpretive "cultural turn," both of which have brought analytic rigor to these earlier formulations. Nevertheless, contemporary approaches still tend to offer relatively simple and unidimensional conceptions of nationalism that fail to explain diverse policy responses in the face of common external economic phenomena. This constitutes a major challenge across a range of disciplines, as current approaches may generate misleading explanations of economic policy processes and inaccurate predictions about ensuing regulatory and market outcomes. This Element offers an alternative approach that historically

---

[17] Kindleberger, Charles. 1969. *Six Lectures on Direct Investment*, New Haven, CT: Yale University Press, 145 (cited in Kobrin, 1987: 610; see also Wellhausen, 2014). Theodore Moran similarly argued that "politics of economic nationalism [w]as determined by the interplay of groups pursuing their own interests and their own vision of the national interest" (Moran, 1974: 245).

[18] Johnson, 1965. Cited in Frieden and Lake, 2005: 143

grounds economic nationalism in the sociopolitical processes through which distinct varieties of anti-colonial nationalisms are formed, contested, and institutionalized, as well as in the economic ideas that offer a sense of causality and rationality. Together, these sociopolitical processes and economic ideas co-constitute economic nationalism and give it rigor and meaning.

Agency vs Modularity in the Global Rise of Nationalisms

While economic nationalism is regularly used in scholarly and policy discourse, surprisingly, it is rarely well defined. Remarkably, this definitional lacuna also holds for scholarship on the broader concept of nationalism. It is thus important to establish clear definitions of both of these closely related concepts. Mylonas and Tudor (2023: 4) argue that, despite the dramatic resurgence of nationalism in the second decade of the twenty-first century, "scholars of nationalism are surprisingly inconsistent in their definitional and conceptual approaches," utilizing a wide array of definitions, but often without directly engaging with each other. They offer a path forward by describing nationalism as having three core attributes: (1) an intersubjective recognition and celebration of an "imagined community" as a locus of loyalty and solidarity; (2) a drive for sovereign self-rule over a distinct territory that is pursued by a significant segment of a group's elite; and (3) a repertoire of symbols, practices and narratives that embody the nation (Mylonas and Tudor, 2023: 5). I build on this framing that centers Benedict Anderson's (2006) notion of nation as "imagined community," the importance of territorial sovereignty and elite control (which is especially important in the case of oil in Brazil), and the centrality of cultural symbols and narratives (particularly striking in the case of manufacturing in India).

In order to develop a working definition of *economic* nationalism, I couple this attention to imagined community, territoriality, symbolism, and narratives with what Rawi Abdelal describes as the intersubjective "content" of nationalism. Abdelal (2001: 1) defines nationalism as a "proposal of the content of national identity" that reflects society's collective – though often contested – interpretations of the social meaning of the nation, the path it should follow, and the policies that societal actors believe will achieve those goals. I build on Abdelal and Mylonas and Tudor by defining economic nationalism as an elite project of sovereign control of physical territory, society, and economy through a constructed notion of community animated by a set of historically rooted symbols, narratives, and practices. To paraphrase Abdelal, economic nationalism is an attempt to link the idea of a nation to specific *economic* goals. These goals are defined in relation to both: retrospectively, to a sense of national history, and prospectively, to a sense of national purpose. This framework for understanding the relationship between policy preferences and economic nationalism provides significant analytic room for agency and contestation. While the social meaning of nationalism is intersubjectively held, the "content" of every national "proposal" is hotly debated and contested by groups and individuals across a given society. There are always competing nationalist projects with political battles determining which will prevail.

Finally, nationalisms do not emerge within a vacuum; they arise in interaction with and often in opposition to other nationalisms in the international state system and the global political economy. Nationalisms are relational and are often imagined having an "other" both within and outside of the state (for example, in India, Hindu nationalists as distinct from secular nationalists often see both Indian Muslims as well as the "West" as others). It is variation in this "content" as deployed by competing nationalist actors that gives rise to contestation between competing national goals and identities in a given society as well as across countries. This variation in content and contestation ultimately produces differences in economic policies and market outcomes.

There is a tension between the unique cultural construct of the nation that nationalist actors must create to successfully oppose the imperialist "other," and the homogenizing forces of the global political economy. Brazil and Indian nationalists were not alone in their efforts to imagine a unified nation in the late nineteenth century. After all, this was the period of the first globalization, a time when the Westphalian system of nation-states was coming into being. The global political environment was characterized by nationalist struggles to consolidate territories, peoples, and economies in Africa, Asia, Europe, and Latin America and the Caribbean. This was also the moment when "late-developing" states such as the United States and Germany sought to establish domestic industrial capacity within the wider institutional context of globally dominant British manufacturing and a free trade regime enforced by the combined might of British capital, the British navy, and British theories of classical political economy.

These efforts by late-developing states provided institutional templates for the colonies that Anderson (2006 [1983]) has referred to as "modular," providing a valuable framework for the construction of nationalist proposals. Anderson showed that nationalist imaginaries cannot be analyzed in isolation; they are part of wider sociohistoric dynamics in both their material and cultural dimensions. Economic nationalisms are products of global economic and technological processes as well as the cultural meanings and practices that accompany them. Anderson identified the new discourse of nationalism and the mechanisms through which it was transplanted across space and time, allowing nascent conceptions of nationalism to spread through Asia, Europe, and Latin America in the mid to late nineteenth century. Brazil and India were no exceptions: the processes occurring within India and Brazil in the late nineteenth century cannot be divorced from political developments in other regions of the world. Indeed, anti-colonial nationalist figures were keen participants in global circuits in the early-mid-twentieth century from metropolitan locations such as London, Paris, New York, and Berlin to new convening spaces in the Global South such as Arusha and Bandung (cf. Getachew, 2019). Nevertheless, despite the availability of nationalist ideas in the global environment, the construction of Indian economic nationalism, for example, required strategic efforts by emergent nationalist actors to reformulate "modular" ideas for the Indian context. This is the very definition of agency – "the capacity to transpose and extend schemas to new contexts" – that Sewell (1992: 19) argues is required to facilitate structural transformation.

Thus, despite its attractiveness, Goswami (2002: 780) suggests that modular diffusion may be conceptually delinked from the material context of new socioeconomic relations of late nineteenth-century global capitalist production. While Anderson's (2006 [1983]) modular nationalism and theory of nations as imagined communities provide rich insights, they do so at the cost of privileging 'subjective' cultural accounts over 'objective' material explanations. Anderson's (2006 [1983]) emphasis on the subjective is strategic – aiming to correct what he perceived as overly positivistic understandings of the nation through a discursive approach that revealed the subjectivity of nationalism – but his modular approach may nevertheless universalize mimetic processes. This approach risks sacrificing the context-specificity arising from "[material] sociohistorical processes and institutional constraints that attend the production and circulation of meaning" (Goswami 2002: 780). The material and cultural dimensions of sociohistorical processes require equal analytic weight.

While this Element challenges the structural-material assumptions that underpin dominant conceptions of economic interests and policy preferences, the framework that is developed avoids privileging culture over materiality by recognizing the duality of subjective-cultural and objective-material determinants of preferences in shaping the institutional foundations of nationalism in late colonial India and early independent Brazil. Sewell's (1992) theory of duality facilitates a conception of structure as simultaneously material and cultural. For example, it stresses the importance of agency in understanding how Indian actors both interpreted nationalist ideas that they were exposed to in their reading or travels to Europe and East Asia through their own sociohistorical lens and then reformulated these models to the Indian political-economic context, and how Brazilian elites similarly struggled to distinguish their identities from Europe. This agency-oriented approach to nationalism challenges not only Anderson's modularity but also the world polity approach of Meyer et al. (1997). The world polity perspective suggests that ideas diffuse via mimetic processes through elite networks and are adopted wholesale by recipients. The contrasting Brazilian and Indian cases provide a direct empirical challenge to this view (see also Go, 2021).

Indeed, Getachew (2019) provides one of the most powerful articulations of this alternate perspective highlighting the agency of anti-colonial nationalists. She challenges the standard liberal account of decolonization that sees the transition from empire to independent nation and the concomitant expansion of international society to include new postcolonial states "as a seamless and inevitable development" (Getachew, 2019: 14). This conventional view of decolonization sees anticolonial nationalists utilizing the language of liberal self-determination associated with Woodrow Wilson and, like Meyer et al. (1997) would hold, mimicking the existing institutional forms of the nation-state. Getachew argues that characterizing decolonization "as a process of [mimetic] diffusion, in which a gradual 'Westernization' of the world took place, blunts anticolonial nationalism's radical challenge to the four-century-long project of European imperial expansion." However, "Rather than a seamless and inevitable transition from empire to nation, anticolonial nationalists refigured decolonization as a radical rupture – one that required a wholesale transformation of the colonized and a reconstitution of the international order" (Getachew, 2019:16). Instead, anti-colonial economic nationalists such as W.E.B DuBois, Kwame Nkrumah, Julius Nyere, George Padmore, and Eric Williams sought to challenge the entrenched inequality of the international system through processes of "worldmaking." Nkrumah articulated this inequality in stark neocolonial terms, highlighting the widely held concern that foreign interests sought to continue to exploit the labor force and natural resources of newly independent countries: "practically all our natural resources, not to mention trade, shipping, banking, building . . . have remained in the hands of foreigners seeking to enrich alien investors, and to hold back local economic initiative" (cited in Getachew, 2019). These new leaders sought to upend this unequal global economic structure by gaining sovereign control of their national economies.

Getachew (2019) thus shows how, contrary to the view of economic nationalism as autarkic, anti-colonial nationalists in Africa and the Caribbean sought to reform, rather than reject, the unequal international system through processes of "worldmaking." These included an array of institutional innovations such as the formation of regional economic federations in Africa and the Caribbean. Anti-colonial figures such as Michael Manley also participated in the development of broader formations of postcolonial solidarity such as the New International Economic Order (NIEO). These would serve as bulwarks against neo-imperialism, including forms of neo-imperialism carried out by new instruments of postwar empire: international institutions that facilitate unfettered capital flows as well as the organization that replaced the trading companies of the previous era by embodying private foreign capital in the newly decolonized world, the multinational corporation.

Advancing New Conceptions of Economic Nationalism: Content and Contestation

There has been a revival of literature on economic nationalism over the past two decades. These works have in common a rejection of simplistic views associated with earlier, often narrowly materialistic and economistic, literatures discussed in the previous section. This new scholarship began with an initial wave of work in international political economy that challenged the "end of history" notion that neoliberalism and globalization had rendered economic nationalism obsolete (Helleiner, 2002; Helleiner and Pickel, 2005). Instead, these scholars showed how economic nationalism was not necessarily about protectionism, but in fact could be consistent with economic liberalization of the form that swept through the developing (and industrialized) world in the 1980s and 1990s. This was followed by a more recent round of scholarship that went further in highlighting, often in similarly counterintuitive and surprising ways, the historical importance and continued legacy of anti-colonial nationalisms of the 1930s–1970s. For example, Slobodian (2018) showed how the perceived threat of anti-colonial nationalism to the liberal international economic order prompted the genesis of neoliberal ideas in the 1930s by reactionary intellectuals associated with the Walter Lippman Colloquium and the Mont Pelerin Society who sought to "encase" global markets through international law. These important scholarly developments are further elaborated next.

The revival of the literature on economic nationalism in the early 2000s showed how economic nationalism remained a useful analytic concept in the context of globalization and neoliberalism, despite weaknesses in earlier formulations. Helleiner (2002) challenged the conventional wisdom that "economic nationalism is an outdated ideology in this age of globalization and economic liberalization ... [an] assertion [that] usually assumes that the ideology of economic nationalism has a coherent nonliberal policy program which governments no longer endorse." He also rejected the assumption that the 1980s–2000s were "uniformly liberal," given the heterodox path of countries like China (cf. Weber, 2021). Helleiner did so by making two key claims about the nature of economic nationalism in the late twentieth and early twenty-first centuries. First, he argued that economic nationalism is not simply a form of protectionism or strand of statist realism, but is best defined by its nationalist content, a position that resonates with Abdelal (2001). Second, Helleiner showed how contemporary economic nationalism can be compatible with a range of policy approaches and projects, including liberal ones. Economic nationalism thus remains both powerful as an ideology and ambiguous with respect to policy goals and cultural content.[19]

Helleiner further posited economic nationalism as a rival to economic liberalism and neoliberalism in the wake of the late twentieth-century collapse of communism and the Marxist political project. In the nineteenth century, economic liberalism was a powerful force with Marxism and economic nationalism as its main rivals. Yet, as illustrated earlier by the Johnson and Kindleberger quotes, economic nationalism became the subject of analytic confusion in much of the twentieth century, ranging from characterizations of irrational protectionism to conflations of statism with nationalism. The latter view sought to locate "state-centric realism" in a tradition dating back to seventeenth- to eighteenth-century mercantilism (Gilpin, 1987). Yet others challenged this perspective, arguing that statism is about state interests as separate from society, and social distributions of power, while economic nationalism is about the role of national identities and economic ideas inspired by nationalist beliefs in shaping economic policy (Abdelal, 2001). These beliefs should be clearly defined before examining "foreign economic policy preference theoretically and empirically" (Shulman, 2000).

Recent literature has sharpened the economic nationalism analytic by showing how traditional conceptions ignore nationalist content. Helleiner (2002) argues that much of the problem can be traced back to (mis)readings of the seminal work of Friedrich List. List (1841 [1904]) was best known for his arguments in favor of infant industry protection. However, what was less well-known was that List himself did not define economic nationalism in policy terms but rather in terms of the "nationalist theoretical content of his ideas" (Helleiner, 2002). List stressed nationalism as key to his arguments in *National System of Political Economy* and was critical of the "dead materialism" of classical (liberal) political economists in their failure to take nationalism seriously, instead of focusing on either individuals or humanity as a whole.

The goal of this work was to show that, contra the idea that economic nationalism was an outdated ideology in the context of the collapse of communism and the rise (and seemingly inevitable domination) of globalization and economic liberalization, economic nationalism remained a powerful force in shaping economic policy, albeit often in radically different directions.

---

[19] Indeed, consistent with this Element's identification of different varieties of anti-colonial economic nationalisms in postwar Brazil and India, Helleiner identifies four strands of economic nationalism in the nineteenth century: infant industry, macroeconomic activism, autarchic economic nationalism, and liberal economic nationalism.

Economic nationalism does not necessarily represent illiberal policies that fewer governments appeared to endorse in the era of globalization and liberalization. Instead, some contemporary strands of economic nationalism may run counter to economic liberalization, such as what Helleiner refers to in recently published work as "neo-mercantilist economic nationalism" (Helleiner, 2021) while others may (seemingly paradoxically) not.

Anti-Colonial Economic Nationalism and the Roots of Neoliberalism

This new strand of critical literature on economic nationalism thus gained traction as a response to neoliberalism and globalization. Indeed, the relationship between economic nationalism and neoliberalism has an important genealogy. This is important to present. First, to understand the interrelated set of political and ideational developments that led to the rise of different economic nationalisms in the mid-century. Second, to make sense of the ways in which those economic nationalisms shaped the later rise of neoliberalism in the late twentieth century (and the return of economic nationalism in the twenty-first). In *Globalists: The End of Empire and the Birth of Neoliberalism*, Quinn Slobodian (2018) shows how anti-colonial economic nationalism lies at the root of neoliberalism itself. Slobodian argues that it was the fear of rising economic nationalism that served as the central motivating force for early neoliberals such as Freidrich von Hayek, Ludwig von Mises, Wilheim Röpke, and other members of the Walter Lippman Colloquium and the Mont Pelerin Society. Their ideas were explicitly developed in reaction to the perceived threat of rising economic nationalism, impending democracy, and statist economic planning in Eastern Europe and the decolonizing world. Further, and paradoxically, they sought to constrain demands for economic and political sovereignty in colonized spaces by privileging the sovereignty of multinational firms and private capital flows. Their proposal was to "encase" the global economy through an international legal architecture that would supersede the dangerous inclinations of soon-to-be independent states that were challenging forms of neocolonialism that Getachew (2019) and others discuss.

Meeting and writing in Europe in the midst of rising fascism in the 1930s, these architects of neoliberalism believed that "The greatest danger [facing the world] is the new business cycle policy: the policy of economic autonomy, the policy of economic nationalism, combined with the planned economy and autarchy" (Slobodian, 2018: 21–22). A key element of their concerns lay with the new techniques of economic governance that were rising to the fore during this period, not least Keynesian macroeconomic management as well as New

Deal-style industrial, infrastructural, and social welfare policies. These technocratic tools of economic planning offered new ways of "seeing" the economy and thus rendering economy and society manipulable in ways that could conform to the needs and demands of anti-colonial actors (Scott, 1998; Mitchell, 2002). Hayek and others feared that "Seeing economics through statistics and cycles had fostered fantasies of management at the scale of the nation that threatened to pave the way to global disorder" (Slobodian, 2018: 89). The underlying issues in intellectual debates such as the socialist calculation controversy, as well as much of Hayek's critiques of "the impossibility of planning," were directed toward averting what they saw as an impending disaster of economic planning (Hayek, 1937, 1945). The market was seen as a superior means of coordinating economic activity. The key innovation that Hayek and others proposed was to use the supranational legal system to constrain the scope of economic management by sovereign states, thus enabling capital to move freely but also limiting the possibilities for more equitable and democratically governed national and global systems (Slobodian, 2018).

The neoliberal critique of planning was made not only on technical economic grounds but also on the basis of politics. German economist Wilhelm Röpke, for example, offered a highly instrumentalized view of economic nationalism as a cynical outcome of powerful domestic economic interests that had effectively captured politicians. This view mirrors some of the later work by economic historians of state-multinational relations and foreign investment policy such as Charles Kindleberger and Theodore Moran. It also anticipates public choice theory of later "Virginia School" neoliberal thinkers such as political economist James Buchanan. Röpke further suggested that economic nationalism was fundamentally empty: It was merely a political strategy of providing interest groups with labor protections, trade subsidies, and tax breaks in exchange for their political support (Slobodian, 2018: 114). Indeed, Slobodian shows how Röpke sought to turn the anti-colonial nationalist critique upside down by insisting that, contra the views of figures like Kwame Nkrumah, "capitalism itself was anti-imperialist ... [arguing] that the doctrine of geopolitics frequently confused the principles of imperium and dominium." Instead, Röpke held that "political domination (imperium) is necessary for economic exploitation (dominium)" under economic nationalism (Slobodian, 2018: 116). These discourses on the content of economic nationalism and the contestation they engendered were characteristic of the interwar period when demands for decolonization became impossible for the colonial powers to ignore. For many scholars of comparative and international political economy, making sense of these debates turned on the ways in which material interests and nationalist beliefs might shape the policymaking process.

4 Structural Similarities, Sociohistorical Differences: Brazil and India Compared

Theories of economic nationalism have become a mainstay of historical sociology, comparative and international political economy, and international management (Gilpin, 1975, 1987; Vernon, 1971; Abdelal, 2001; Helleiner, 2002). However, these theories say little about how differences in the sociohistorical origins of nationalist beliefs shape political conflicts and variation in industry-level policy outcomes. This Element identifies the sources of contrasting beliefs in economic nationalism that shaped postwar industrial policy and firm strategy in the early periods of state formation and market construction in late nineteenth-century Brazil and India. Further, while colonial legacies are central to the theory of economic nationalism proposed in this Element, cross-national variation in approaches to foreign firms cannot be easily dismissed by reference to Brazil's and India's contrasting colonial experiences. India entered the postwar period after a long independence struggle and so might have been expected to promote domestic ownership and control of manufacturing industries like automobiles, yet surprisingly granted the most nefarious of foreign firms – the oil multinationals – major concessions and allowed them to establish and retain dominant positions in the strategically important petroleum sector. By contrast, Brazil achieved independence decades earlier with little struggle against its Portuguese colonizers, and postwar policymakers welcomed multinational corporations in manufacturing industries like automobiles. Nationalist demands were largely satisfied as long as production took place within Brazilian borders. However, political battles raged over economic nationalist concerns in natural resources like oil and strenuous efforts were made to exclude foreign firms. What explains this puzzling pattern of cross-country and cross-industry variation?

India and Brazil serve as excellent comparative cases to interrogate competing theories of policy preferences and economic nationalism.[20] First, both countries entered the postwar period intent on pursuing policies that departed from the liberal free trade consensus of the pre-Depression era. Both economies had been oriented around primary commodity exports throughout the nineteenth century – cotton, jute, and tea in India, and coffee, sugar, and rubber in

---

[20] The works of Peter Evans (1995) and Atul Kohli (2004) are cornerstones in the field of comparative political economy of development. While both used South Korea as a prototypical case of the successful "developmental state," epitomizing "embedded autonomy" for Evans (1995) and the balance of class power for Kohli (2004), the strengths of these analyses were revealed in their treatment of the complex "intermediate" cases of Brazil and India. The nuances of these cases provided the test of their analytic strength of their theories, yet this comparison has rarely been revisited by political scientists, sociologists, or scholars of international management.

Brazil – and both countries were embedded in mercantilist trade relationships dominated by British merchant firms and the British state. A structural analysis would begin by deducing policy actors' preferences in each country from their common structural positions (Gourevitch, 1986). Yet India and Brazil occupied similar structural locations in the global economy in the period leading up to the Second World War that marked the beginning of their postwar industrialization drive. Indeed, key leaders such as Getulio Vargas and Jawaharlal Nehru explicitly articulated concerns about the subordinate positions that their countries occupied in the global order. Thus, a conventional structural analysis would do little to explain the observed variation in Brazil's and India's policy positions.

Second, policymakers in both India and Brazil found themselves in similar macroeconomic positions at the end of the Second World War as they struggled with fiscal constraints arising from their weak balance of payments positions. By 1945, both countries had accumulated large war-related foreign exchange surpluses, only to see their current account balances turn quickly and dangerously negative shortly thereafter. Brazil amassed US$600 million of reserves through raw material export receipts, import controls, and shortages during the Second World War, which allowed the government to adopt an open import regime. Brazilian consumers responded accordingly, with motor vehicles and auto parts leading an explosion of import demand. However, by the end of 1947 foreign exchange reserves accumulated during the war were exhausted, creating fiscal imbalances as import demand exceeded foreign currency availability. An overvalued *cruzeiro* exacerbated the hard currency shortage and led to licensing and hard currency rationing that favored capital goods and discriminated against 'non-essential' consumer durables such as automobiles.[21] Crucially, balance of payments concerns not only arose from booming imports, but also from the fact that Brazil's trade surpluses and monetary reserves were held in European currencies that were not readily convertible in the aftermath of the war and the destruction of the major European economies. This was a significant constraint, as scarce US dollars were needed for most imports (Shapiro, 1994: 30). This made a deep impression on Brazilian policymakers. They interpreted this crisis as an outcome of Brazil's geopolitical weakness, marginal position in the hierarchy of nations, and structural dependence on hegemonic economic powers. This combination fueled a particular strain of economic nationalism that was driven by feelings of dependency.

India similarly emerged from the Second World War with strong current account surpluses. Sterling balances held by the Reserve Bank peaked at

---

[21] There was high consumer demand for automobiles, but auto imports placed a taxing toll on reserve position. This underpinned part of the rationale for the focus on developing an automobile industry by Brazilian policymakers.

17.3 million pounds in April 1946, and India held a whopping 1.7 billion pounds of Great Britain's external liabilities, more than 50% of the UK's total foreign obligations. However, the British refused to honor their fiscal obligations as their grip on the colony weakened, thus negating a balance sheet that had a strong surplus. This placed India in a tight fiscal position right at the cusp of achieving independence. As in Brazil, British capacity to refuse to honor their obligations highlighted India's weak geopolitical status. It was clear to Indian policymakers that their subordination to global powers persisted despite the triumph of independence in August 1947. Thus, the material conditions that characterized both countries were also similar, as were the economic and geopolitical dynamics through which macroeconomic pressures in Brazil and India arose. However, as we will see, these similar experiences of structural subordination nevertheless had different implications for the type of nationalist beliefs that emerged and became dominant in postwar economic policy.

The Constructivist Alternative and the Role of Ideas

Constructivist approaches in sociology and political science have been advanced to challenge structural and materialist theories of the political economy of the policymaking process. Scholars working in this tradition have empirically established the analytic value of ideational analysis by convincingly demonstrating how policy changes cannot be explained by structural and material factors alone (Dobbin, 1994; Abdelal, Blyth and Parsons, 2010). Instead, they have argued that policymaking is shaped by the role of ideas, which operate, much like Max Weber (1946) proposed, as "switchmen [that] determined the tracks along which action has been pushed by the dynamic of interest." This Element builds on this scholarship through an analysis of the relationship between economic ideas and nationalist belief systems. However, it goes beyond this work by highlighting how nationalist beliefs generate distinct patterns of contestation between competing economic theories and policy ideas and produce divergent policy outcomes. Much as the previous section showed how Brazil and India occupied similar structural positions, so too were policy elites in India and Brazil exposed to similar economic theories and industrial development strategies. Yet they interpreted and contested these ideas differently and as a result, pursued sharply contrasting policy paths. Why was this so?

Brazil's and India's compromised macroeconomic positions certainly had important implications for how policymakers "puzzled" over competing approaches to the regulation of foreign capital.[22] Prevailing neoclassical economic

---

[22] Hugh Heclo offers an alternative perspective on politics within the state that rests on the role of ideas, suggesting that "Politics finds its sources not only in power but also in uncertainty-men

theories provided economic planners with compelling rationales for promoting FDI as a means to simultaneously achieve the goals of macroeconomic stability and industrial development. These orthodox theories suggested that foreign firms could bring in desperately needed hard currency to set up enterprises that would produce for export markets, thus bolstering the capacity to earn valuable foreign exchange. This strategy was predicated on the existence of factor price differentials that lie at the core of neoclassical trade theory: poor countries with large pools of low-cost labor had a comparative advantage in the production of labor-intensive goods. According to classical conceptions of comparative advantage, these countries would benefit from engaging in trade with industrialized countries that produced capital-intensive manufactured goods (Lewis, 1954; Bhagwati and Desai, 1970). This approach had clear implications for the regulation of foreign investment, aptly captured in Nobel Prize–winning St Lucian economist Sir Arthur Lewis' call for "industrialization by invitation."[23]

Yet an alternative set of heterodox economic theories was being developed in this early postwar period that causally linked these macroeconomic imbalances to excessive reliance on imports of manufactured consumer and capital goods, which policymakers, analysts, and observers in both countries attributed to their underdeveloped industrial sectors. This underdevelopment was believed to be the outcome of developing countries' structural dependence on industrialized countries for capital, technology, and manufactured goods. This was the same type of structural dependence that Third World leaders like Nkrumah and Nyere as well as Nehru and Vargas sought to overcome. The policy solution was to boost domestic manufacturing efforts in industries where production output would substitute for imported goods to reduce hard currency outflows.[24]

This was the central rationale of the alternative development model of state-directed import substituting industrialization (ISI). The ISI model was spreading across the developing world in the 1950s and 1960s, due in part to the work of economists such as Raul Prebisch at the United Nations Economic

---

collectively wondering what to do ... Governments not only 'power' ... they also puzzle. Policymaking is a form of collective puzzlement on society's behalf" (cited in Hall, 1993: 275).

[23] Lewis, Arthur W. (1950). Industrial Development in the Caribbean. Port of Spain: Caribbean Commission. (A reprint of "Industrial Development in Puerto Rico" Caribbean Economic Review, Vol. L, Nos. 1 and 2; 1949; and "The Industrialisation of the British West Indies," *Caribbean Economic Review*, Vol. II, No. 1, May 1950.). See also Girvan, Norman. (2005) "W.A. Lewis, the Plantation School, and Dependency: An Interpretation." *Social and Economic Studies*, September 2005, Vol. 54, No. 3, Special Issue on Sir Arthur Lewis, Part I (September 2005), pp. 198–221.

[24] Attempts to simultaneously increase foreign exchange inflows by exports entered the policy discourse later as the ISI model was initially fairly silent on the export issue. This is the subject of much of the voluminous literature that later emerged in the 1980s, 1990s, and 2000s, comparing Latin American ISI with East Asian ELI (export led industrialization).

Commission for Latin America (ECLA) (Prebisch, 1950; Hirschman, 1968).[25] Arguments in favor of ISI received significant intellectual support from dependency theory, an influential set of ideas that suggested that developing countries are trapped in fundamentally exploitative relations with industrialized countries (Prebisch, 1950, 1959; Singer, 1950; Gunder Frank, 1966; Cardoso and Felletto, 1979).[26]

Dependency theory was built on a core-periphery model of global capitalism where persistent underdevelopment in the Third World was the outcome of structural dependence on industrialized countries for capital, technology, and manufactured goods.[27] This model of the global capitalist system was self-reinforcing. Raul Prebisch and his fellow economists at UNECLA analyzed commodity trade data, including copper exports from Chile where UNECLA was based, to show that over time, the prices of primary products that were largely exported to the "core" by countries in the "periphery" declined relative to the prices of manufacturing goods that developing countries imported from the industrialized world. As a result, countries that were primarily commodity producing faced declining terms of trade that limited their development prospects.[28] Rising productivity gains from technological change thus were unevenly distributed across the global economy through the mechanism of international trade. Most of the gains accrued to countries in the industrialized "core" with minimal benefits flowing to countries in the underdeveloped "periphery."

This dynamic was deemed to be a structural feature of the global economy from which the mode of escape was through the aforementioned strategy of import substituting industrial development. Addressing the underlying macroeconomic weaknesses that characterized most developing countries coupled with the structural reality of unequal exchange in international trade underpinned the need to gain access to manufacturing technologies that were held by foreign firms. The ISI model duly spread and was adopted, albeit not blindly, by most newly independent states around the world.[29] This theoretically informed

---

[25] Note that the intellectual legacy that rationalizes infant industry protection goes back much earlier to Alexander Hamilton and Friedrich List.

[26] This view, it is worth noting, is consistent with nineteenth-century theory of the economic drain formulated by Dadabhai Naoroji in India.

[27] Different strands of dependence theory developed in different parts of the world over the 1950s, 1960s, and 1970s, emphasizing different analytical approaches and drawing on different intellectual traditions from structural (e.g. Raul Prebisch and Celso Furtado) to neo-Marxist perspectives (e.g. Samir Amin and Paul Baran), among others (e.g. Caribbean plantation school). Nevertheless, they had key elements in common, particularly a historical analytic approach and a focus on structural constraints on production. For excellent reviews see Heller et al. (2009); Kvangraven (2021, 2023).

[28] This argument is captured in the Prebisch-Singer hypothesis.

[29] This dynamic in many ways foreshadowed the development and adoption of neoliberal economic development policies in the 1980s and 1990s. Neoliberal policy diffusion followed the

imperative to industrialize, and the need for foreign capital and technology to do so, had crucial implications for the ownership and control of industry, which would lie at the center of contrasting policy preferences in India and Brazil.

A crucial challenge that both countries faced as they attempted to promote domestic industry was the superior technological and organizational capabilities and established market power of large multinational firms. Like other countries in the new postwar "periphery," India and Brazil sought to rapidly industrialize at the precise historical moment when FDI was taking off and the multinational corporation was emerging as a powerful new organizational phenomenon in the global economy (cf. Wilkins, 1970; see also Hyman, 1960; Vernon, 1971; Fagre and Wells, 1982). This period of aggressive outward expansion of multinational corporations was led by American firms in the wake of the Second World War. The destruction of European and Japanese industry coupled with the dismantling of colonial empires provided American multinationals with enhanced access to a wide array of new markets. The US government actively encouraged private American firms to invest overseas and used its growing postwar status as global hegemon to pressure foreign countries to create investment regulations that were amenable to US multinational expansion.

These US government policies and concomitant multinational firm strategies were further facilitated by the rise of the liberal Bretton Woods international financial institutions. The IMF and the World Bank became major sources of development finance that was conditioned on accepting orthodox policy advice. Crucially, these loan conditionalities increasingly demanded open investment environments, limiting the industrial policy space available to developing countries seeking to build their economies (Gallagher, 2005).[30] As a result, US private investment rose dramatically from US$11.8 billion in 1950 to US

---

perceived failures of ISI models. The associated economic crises in the 1970s and early 1980s were accompanied by other legitimizing public policies and global norms, which sociologists have posited as an example of the mimetic isomorphism of globalization (Fourcade-Gourinchas and Babb, 2001; Henisz, Zelner and Guillen, 2005; Dobbin, Simmons and Garrett, 2007). However, while the diffusion of ISI may seem to fit the "world society" model (Meyer et al., 1997), this Element argues that these ideas were interpreted, strategically reformulated and deployed in different ways based on local sociopolitical and historical contexts (Go, 2008, 2013) as well as (seemingly paradoxically) through the radical cosmopolitan internationalism of many anti-colonial nationalists (Getachew, 2021). This is demonstrated through the different ways in which FDI was regulated in India and Brazil within an otherwise similar ISI "policy paradigm" (Hall, 1993).

[30] While IMF and World Bank conditionalities were not as stringent nor strictly enforced in the postwar era (1945–1977) as in the post-oil crisis period as the Washington Consensus began to take hold (1977 onward), the Bank and the Fund still tended to push for open market policies. This is evidenced by India's 1966 World Bank program (cf. Chaudry et al., 2004; Mukherji, 2012).

$29.7 billion in 1959. As will be seen next, Latin American countries had long been open to American capital since the late nineteenth century and in the postwar moment were especially receptive to US MNCs, and US private investment in the region rose accordingly from US$4.6 billion to US$9 billion during this period (Sikkink, 1991: 46).

This geopolitical dimension of foreign investment brought the relationship between multinational corporations and the state to the fore. As discussed in Section 2, conventional perspectives from international economics offered rationalist conceptualizations of multinational firms as a strategy of transnational capital seeking higher returns on firm-specific assets such as proprietary technology or brand name (Caves, 1996). Dissatisfaction with this perspective led an interdisciplinary set of scholars in the emerging field of international business to push further on the question of why multinational firms enter overseas markets, devoting particular analytic attention to the role that states played in the transnational expansion of capital.

One of the leaders of this new field was economist Raymond Vernon. In Vernon's perspective, national governments played crucial roles in enabling multinational corporations to enter new spaces. He colorfully argued that "foreign investors [especially] in raw materials take the plunge into the dark and chilly waters of a less developed country" because of the incentives that host countries offer. Vernon challenged the assumption, implicit in Marxist dependency theories, that multinational giants enter developing countries wielding overwhelming structural power derived from their technological superiority and deep pockets that enable them to run roughshod over developing country governments, reaping vast profits while exploiting workers and destroying the environment. Vernon turned this perspective on its head.

In addition, Vernon not only asserted that multinational behavior was a function of the inducements offered by host governments, he further argued that power relations between foreign capital and the state were not static; they were dynamic. The multinational firm disproportionately bore the upfront risk of entering a new country by expending significant upfront capital to establish its operations in an unfamiliar and uncertain market. Yet once a multinational's investment was sunk, it became captive to the host government. Vernon thus famously claimed that the initial agreement "obsolesced" even as the ink on the contract dried, and the power of the host government grew relative to the multinational (Vernon, 1971: 52).

Vernon is credited with developing the theory of the "obsolescing bargain," but he was not alone in identifying a dynamic relationship between states and multinational firms. Economic historian Theodore Moran similarly argued that there was a clear shift in bargaining power between multinational corporations and developing countries, based on his influential study of foreign investment in the Chilean copper industry. He claimed that the

> sanctity of contract (together with the paraphernalia of 99-year concessions and 20-year government [investment] guarantees of "inviolability") served the function of attempting to cement the relationship between foreign investor and host government on the initial favorable terms to the foreigner. But ... ceteris did not long remain paribus, sanctity of contract ... was steadily "violated" by "undependable Latins" no less than by "untrustworthy Arabs" and other "firebrand nationalists" in a process that reflected frustration about the original terms and shifts in relative bargaining power. (Moran, 1971: 10)

The interdisciplinary work of scholars like Vernon and Moran significantly bolstered the nascent field of international business, which emerged in business schools as response to the rise of the multinational corporation as a new organizational entity in the globalizing postwar economy. Their research added much-needed historical and political economic analysis of power relations between states and multinationals to otherwise acontextual economic analysis of the global economy as constituted by trade and investment flows disembodied from geopolitical dynamics, institutional structures, and organizational practices. Yet their innovative scholarship nevertheless reinforced a narrowly materialist view of government officials and firm managers as rational actors, even if constrained by the shifting structural conditions in which they found themselves. Further, to the extent that economic nationalism played a role in shaping outcomes, it was only through state actors as protectionist, as the Moran quote suggests. The multinational corporation was still assumed to epitomize the rational calculating economic actor.

This limited perspective was upended by the seminal work of a young Canadian economist named Stephen Hymer. Hymer's key insight was captured in the title of his 1960 dissertation "The International Operations of National Firms." It was both simple and powerful, as his advisor Charles Kindleberger (2002) later reflected. Hymer suggested that firms were fundamentally national, even as they operated in global markets. Suggesting that multinational corporations effectively had a national identity was a radical position. It implied that policymakers were not the only actors that might behave nationalistically; multinational firm managers might be economic nationalists too. Firms could fly flags.

Hymer coupled this core insight with the observation that a crucial difference between portfolio investment and foreign direct investment was the desire of the foreign firm to not only have a claim on profits but to establish managerial control over the overseas operations in which it was invested (Buckley, 2006).

Yet if multinational firm managers were not simply rational profit seekers, but also economic nationalists, it was reasonable to assume that they might use their managerial power for purposes beyond profit maximization. These two elements highlighted core tensions in the operations of the multinational corporation. Multinationals corporations seek to exploit their disproportionate power through establishing monopoly positions in host countries, and further, they might exploit their positions for both economic and political gain. Indeed, as the Cold War deepened in the 1950s, American multinational managers in Brazil and India often saw the success of their firms' investments on the ground as not limited to financial returns but also as serving as a bulwark against the "communist threat," as the coming sections will show. The two objectives were often intertwined.[31]

These insights further entrenched the issue of economic nationalism at the front and center of the analysis of multinational firm behavior in the global economy. This Element now turns to assessing how economic nationalist beliefs manifested in Brazil and India and shaped foreign investment policy outcomes.

5 Historicizing the Colonial Roots of Economic Nationalisms in Brazil and India

Economic nationalism may be defined as "the attempt to link the idea of a nation to specific [economic] goals" (Abdelal, 2001: 1). Nationalism is a "proposal of the content of national identity" that reflects a society's collective interpretations of the social meaning of the nation, the path it should follow, and the policies that societal actors believe will produce the socioeconomic goals that define the national project (Abdelal, 2001: 1; Helleiner, 2002). Thus economic relationships such as the expected effects of FDI on industrial development are deeply embedded in the Brazilian and Indian sociocultural fabric. It is variation in the sociohistorical evolution of these belief systems that shaped differences in Indian and Brazilian actors' preferences for foreign investment. The variation that is generated by these contrasting historical paths is lost in analyses that rely on conceptions of nationalism as a binary variable where *magnitude*, that is, whether countries are "more" or "less" nationalist, rather than *content* of nationalism, is seen as determining regulatory, strategic, and ultimately market outcomes. Instead, this Element analyzes variation in the social meaning of

---

[31] For example, during a trip to the United States to meet with potential investment partners, leading Indian businessman GD Birla noted that "Businessmen here are generally sympathetic to India. They realize with China gone and other parts of Asia in turmoil, India is the only country that contributes towards peace in Asia." Reported in the *Hindustan Times* piece, "Foreign Capital for India. Nehru's Statements welcomed in the USA. Mr Birla's Impressions" (May 23, 1949).

Economic Nationalisms in Brazil and India

economic nationalism though institutionalized legacies of political conflicts in each country context.

The Element reveals major differences in the content of the distinct economic nationalist belief systems that became dominant in postwar India and Brazil.[32] These beliefs explain why policy and business actors in these countries displayed such contrasting stances toward FDI in the immediate postwar period. Policymakers' preferences toward foreign investment in both Brazil and India were certainly "nationalist." However, "economic nationalism" manifested in strikingly different ways across key industries with major implications for the patterns of market development and industrialization that followed. This Element will show that these are due to differences in the social, political, and economic experiences of actors in each country.

Colonial experience and the state-and market-building processes that began in the late nineteenth century played a major role in the construction of economic nationalism in both countries. Indian economic nationalism was strongly anti-imperial, having emerged as a counterpoint to colonial rule after the British Crown took direct control of the colony from the East India Company in 1857. Pre-colonial India was loosely organized under a variety of regional "princely states," many of which were products of the declining Mughal Empire. Much like the East India Company, the British "Raj" functioned by superimposing colonial authority on preexisting structures of political and economic governance that had existed for centuries under pre-European empires (Bayly, 1983). The goal was to facilitate private trade–based commercial extraction through markets that were structured through liberal legal rules of property and contract. British colonial governance was justified in terms of the developmental benefits provided to Indian colonial subjects, exemplified by the annual production of *Moral and Material Reports*.

In India, ideas of economic nationalism began to emerge and coalesce in the late nineteenth century through the work of figures such as Dadabhai Naoroji, M. G. Ranade, and R.C. Dutt.[33] These foundational Indian economic nationalists

---

[32] This distinction goes beyond conceptions of nationalist ideologies that are typically found in literatures on these countries – anti-imperialist Nehruvian statist developmentalism and nationalist-populist *desenvolvimentismo*." Brazilian *Desenvolvimentismo* referred to a set of ideas governing state-led industrialization to promote economic development and raise the national standard of living. It was associated both with the military and the Vargas and Kubitschek regimes in the pre- and immediate postwar periods, and crucially, as Sikkink (1991) argues, had an important populist dimension that was absent in India. Nehruvian "scientific socialism" was a set of beliefs that rose to dominance through contestation with Gandhianism as well as the liberal colonial orthodoxy in the 1930s. It shaped the thinking of Indian nationalists as the country gained independence in 1947, and played a crucial role in policy formulation and debates for the next three decades.

[33] There were even earlier strands of nationalist thinking developed by Marathi intellectuals in the 1850s.

developed a coherent nationalist belief system built on the novel theory of the economic "drain." Drain theory posited specific mechanisms through which the British extracted vast economic resources from India and quantified both the abstract financial losses to the country and the material squalor, poverty, and famines that the Indian people suffered. Crucially for the conceptualization of economic nationalism offered here, colonial extraction was primarily understood in terms of outflows of gold as a means of payment for British manufactured goods, which displaced local artisanal production through the imposition of 'free trade', as well as to repay debts foisted on the colony for infrastructure development, particularly the railroads. As such, despite its connotation, the "drain" did not simply refer to natural resource extraction. It specifically referred to the structure of unequal exchange between the colony and the metropole and the deindustrializing effects it generated, an analytic relationship that anticipated twentieth-century dependency theory. This is an important distinction for the industry-level comparison with Brazil in the postwar period.[34]

The economic ideas that constituted drain theory were explicitly oriented toward promoting industrial development, which Indian economic nationalists believed was the key to modernity. These nationalist beliefs were underpinned by historical narratives of India's glorious artisanal manufacturing tradition that predated the British, which nationalist actors argued was being destroyed by colonial laissez-faire economic policies enforced for the benefit of Lancashire textile producers (Dutt, 1901, 1903). As such, advancing the interests of the Indian nation was seen as a project of *revitalizing* Indian manufacturing. Indian nationalists developed the concept of *swadeshi* or "self-reliance." *Swadeshi* called for the boycott of foreign manufactured goods and the promotion of domestic production to bolster the development of indigenous industry. *Swadeshi* thus entailed a degree of delinking from the imperial West, both the old colonizer in London and rising neo-imperial hegemons such as Germany, Japan, and the United States.[35]

---

[34] The crucial issue is that colonialism was seen as knocking India off its path of "natural" industrial development, not simply as extracting natural resources. It is this derailment that was of chief concern to emerging Indian nationalists. This is why the logic of postindependence industrial policy was to get it back on track, for which foreign capital would be necessary, albeit as a source of technology. This distinction forms the basis for the comparative industry-level argument that is laid out later in the Element.

[35] The roots of *swadeshi* can be traced to as early as 1840s, but these ideas began to gain credence and popularity with an 1870 article in the *Native Opinion* and a series of lectures by Justice Mahadev Govind Ranade in 1872. Swadeshi thus emerged alongside the drain thesis. The idea of *swadeshi* grew vigorously from 1880 to 1895, fueled by the growing market tensions between Indian cotton textiles and those from Lancashire. Eventually, it exploded into acts of widespread social, political, and economic resistance around the turn of the century. *Swadeshi* would continue to be a powerful cultural symbol which became one of the key tools that Mohandas Gandhi would use in mobilizing the nationalist movement across India from the 1920s onward.

Brazil, by contrast, had an entirely different colonial experience, which underpinned different institutional processes of state and market construction, with implications for the development of a distinct variety of economic nationalism. Brazil was a plantation slavery–based agricultural commodity-producing settler colony, as compared to the Indian economy that was based on peasant farming and artisanal production. Brazil had a vast and sparsely populated interior that was weakly governed by a colonial central government comprising local elites. India was densely populated and agrarian, and proto-industrial production was organized through complex social hierarchies and deeply interlinked through goods and credit markets that spanned the subcontinent (and was integrated into global trade circuits) for centuries before the arrival of the Europeans (Bayly, 1983). Indian rulers, whether under the Mughal Empire or quasi-independent "Princely states," saw the British as an external force to be contended with either through peaceably negotiating trade relations or through engaging in war. Crucially, Brazilian governing elites did not view the Portuguese state as an alien imperial power in the way that the Indians perceived the British. In fact, when the Prince Regent Joao was forced to flee Portugal under British protection after Napoleon's invasion in 1807, local landed and merchant elites welcomed his court, which Prince Joao re-established in Rio de Janeiro, transforming the city from a relative backwater to a bustling and cosmopolitan metropolis. Brazil eventually declared itself an independent monarchy in 1822 under Joao's heir, Emperor Dom Pedro I.

Kohli (2004: 133) suggests that the "swift" and "painless" manner in which sovereignty was achieved in Brazil left both nationalist sentiments and political organizations fragmented and with a "weak sense of national purpose." However, independence did not automatically lead to a "strong" centralized state and "clear" national identity. The emperor's administration in Rio de Janeiro, which was quite European and elite, was unable to establish a cohesive national polity – including control over local bosses in Brazil's outer regions – and eventually clashed with a growing military that had stronger social ties within the wider Brazilian society. More fundamentally, Kohli's characterization is representative of much of the literature that conceptualizes nationalism in terms of quantitative magnitude rather than qualitative content. Instead, this Element has argued that economic nationalism is better interpreted in terms of social meaning (Abdelal, 2001; Helleiner, 2002). This further highlights the analytic leverage of industry level comparison between Brazil and India.

As in India, the pursuit of industrial modernity became the center of social and political contestation in Brazil. The emperor's reign coincided with an emerging conflict between the old slave-based sugar and rubber economy in the North-East and North, and the growing coffee and gold industries further south in São Paulo. The monarch had supported the former with mercantilist policies throughout the nineteenth century while the latter was clamoring for free trade to take advantage of Brazil's increasingly dominant position in global coffee production. The Brazilian military, which had been formed to resolve various border disputes with Brazil's neighbors, was instrumental in resolving this conflict. This was the genesis of the Brazilian military's continuous role in politics over the course of the next century, underpinned by a deep concern with sovereignty, territorial integrity, and control.

Brazilian military officers were inculcated with Comte's positivist ideas of science and technology as the basis of progress and saw the new coffee industry and the nascent manufacturing activities that were emerging along with it as more "modern" than the old planter elite associated with Brazil's North-east sugar-slave-rubber complex that had been the mainstay of the economy since the sixteenth century (Kohli, 2004: 135). The military eventually shifted its allegiance, and the monarch was ousted in a coup on November 15, 1889, and forced to return to Portugal as Brazil declared itself a Republic. The military thus played a central role in Brazilian state formation and political governance. As we will see, military logics would become central to the construction of Brazilian economic nationalism, with important implications for the role of FDI in oil.

The relative timing of these political developments in state formation in India and Brazil is worth briefly noting. Just four years after the nascent nationalist movement in India had coalesced as an anti-colonial organizational force with the formation of the Indian National Congress (INC) in 1885, Brazil had already achieved independence and Republican status with little struggle against its former colonial rulers. Brazil's transition from monarchy to republic began what would become a long-standing and increasingly institutionalized relationship between the military and economic elites that would shape the *type* of economic nationalism that would emerge. However, as Kohli (2004) argues, the absence of a significant fight for independence against a colonial oppressor did little to cement a cohesive Brazilian national identity as a counterpoint to European imperialism. This stands in contrast to the anti-colonial nationalism that India's long independence struggle against the British produced. Instead, Brazilian nationalism emerged with the military providing crucial sets of ideas about the nature of the state, which accordingly were largely oriented around national defense.

The Institutionalization of Nationalist Beliefs in Brazil and India

These emerging economic nationalisms had important effects, not least on the type of trade, industrial, and foreign investment policies that the new Brazilian Republic sought to pursue. Topik (1987: 130) suggests that "Rather than viewing foreigners as threats to national sovereignty ... Brazil's dominant class and state administration ... wanted to Europeanize Brazil and believed reliance on world markets was the best way to achieve that."[36] As discussed earlier, the new Brazilian Republic was formed through a close alliance with coffee interests. In addition to supporting new business development around the coffee industry it was also committed to the laissez-faire approach that coffee producers and merchants favored. This led to an expansion of coffee production by opening new lands, attracting European labor, and building railroads to expand production and trade deeper into the rich and fertile São Paulo hinterland.

Railroad expansion in contexts ranging from Europe to the Americas was especially crucial for the consolidation of markets and the state during this period of the late nineteenth century (Dobbin, 1994). The Brazilian state looked abroad for capital and technology, and guaranteed profits to foreign investors. This prompted strong inflows of British as well as American capital fueling rapid growth of the railroad network. The opening of the Santos-Jundai line in 1867 connecting the western hinterland of São Paulo to the sea provided a massive boost to agricultural production in the vast and fertile interior (Hanley, 2005: 3). Coffee production grew rapidly with the number of coffee trees quintupling between 1880 and 1900, making Brazil the largest producer of coffee in the world, accounting for more than 50% of global supply (ibid.). British capital was thus viewed favorably as facilitating development and trade in the São Paulo region that would become the industrial center of twentieth-century Brazil.

By contrast, while British private capital similarly created joint stock companies to build the railroads in India beginning in the mid nineteenth century, they were afforded profit guarantees by the British imperial government, which ultimately were financed through local taxes on colonial subjects. Early Indian nationalists viewed this policy of guaranteed profits as a major source of the "national drain."[37] Further, the railroads were seen as an instrument that facilitated *colonial extraction*, not through removal of natural resources but by extending the reach of British merchant trade deeper into the Indian heartland, further displacing local artisanal production, rather than facilitating *economic development* and *transformation* by opening virgin hinterlands for production

---

[36] Also cited in Kohli (2004: 144).
[37] British private capital also received profit guarantees for railroad investments in Brazil. However, by the turn of the century, the Brazilian state began to find the burden of guaranteeing a minimum rate of return to foreign-owned railroads increasingly onerous and moved to nationalize the railroad but opted to do so by contracting large overseas loans to purchase the railroads outright from their foreign owners rather than arbitrarily confiscating private property (Baer, 2001). The British colonial government also took over the railways in the first few years of the twentieth century, and they were fully nationalized by the independent Indian state in 1951.

and trade, as in Brazil. Indeed, the Governor-General of India, Lord Hardinge, offered support to the railway construction effort claiming that the "plains of Hindosthan offered remarkable facility for building railways which would be of immense value to the commerce, government and military control of the country."[38] The railroads were thus a source of major nationalist agitation and resentment in India stemming from their role in enabling colonial extraction through trade and taxes. They were seen as a symbol of unequal terms of commercial engagement, not as a harbinger of development and modernity as in Brazil and elsewhere in the industrializing world, including the United States.[39]

The utility of the comparison between India and Brazil is further illustrated by the fact that both countries were dealing with the same dominant foreign economic power, albeit under different modes of political control. Many economic historians of Brazil have pointed to the important role of foreign capital in the old Republic,[40] and as in India, private British capital was dominant.[41] However, unlike India where British firms controlled jute, tea, and sugar processing as well as most engineering industries, often to the *exclusion* of indigenous economic actors (Misra, 1999), British capital in Brazil showed little inclination to expand their dominant presence in railroads, shipping, and merchant trade to agricultural processing or manufacturing industry.[42] In fact, manufacturing accounted for just 2% of total British investment in the wider Latin America region and 3% of British capital in Brazil (Evans, 1979: 60; Hanley, 2005; see Table 1). Emerging Brazilian industrialists thus did not share their Indian counterparts' negative historical experience of competition with foreign companies in a discriminatory policy environment controlled by an external imperial power, and so did not perceive foreign firms as impediments to their growth as did their Indian counterparts. Foreign firms held an entirely different social meaning for emerging Brazilian capitalists. This historical difference persisted even when Brazilian firms found themselves in the same

---

[38] Cited in Daniel Thornier, *Investment in Empire*, Philadelphia, 1950, p. 63.

[39] See Ludden (1992) and Goswami (1998) on how the railroads facilitated new market imaginaries in India, which contrasts sharply with Brazil. See also Dobbin (1994), Roy (1997), and Perrow (2002) on the role of railway development as a modernizing force in the United States.

[40] Dean (1969) and Topik (1987) are important proponents of this view. See Hanley (2005: 109) for a partial critique that distinguishes foreign debt financing from equity financing in the turn-of-the-century São Paolo industrial sector, particularly those firms financed by the Bolsa (the nascent Brazilian stock market). There is a long-standing debate in Brazilian historiography around this area that is worthy of future research.

[41] American and other foreign capital became increasingly important in the first few decades of the twentieth century, first in utilities and then increasingly in areas like chemicals.

[42] British ownership of the railroads and shipping firms did facilitate control of merchant trade, and Brazilian commodity exports were used to purchase manufactures from the UK.

Table 1 Distribution of British investment in Brazil, 1875–1913 (% by sector)

	1875	1895	1905	1913
Government loans	66	56	68	47
Railways	21	36	20	23
Public utilities	9	4	5	22
Financial	–	–	1	4
Raw materials	1	1	3	1
Industrial and miscellaneous	3	3	3	3
Total (pounds-sterling)	30,928,000	92,988,000	122,903,000	254,812,000

Source: *Hanley, 2005 Table 4.9*

industry as multinationals during the post–Second World War industrialization boom, as Peter Evans (1979) "triple alliance" has famously shown.[43]

In addition to the different social and cultural meanings ascribed to foreign firms, there were fundamental differences in the collective understanding of the historical roles of the manufacturing industry in India and Brazil. In stark contrast to India, a prevailing belief throughout the nineteenth century was that "industry was 'entirely artificial in Brazil, surviving only at the expense of excessive monetary devaluation and tariff protection'" (Evans, 1979: 64). Much of the Brazilian political elite agreed with both Portuguese mercantilists and British free trade advocates, that "industry on the periphery is unnatural" (Evans, 1979: 64; see also Wirth, 1970: 91). This was precisely the opposite view in India, despite the fact that both countries were perfect examples of "classic dependence" given their structural position in the late nineteenth-century global political economy as subordinate trade partners exchanging primary commodities for British manufactured goods.

This not to say that these ideas that naturalized backwardness were absent in India. India nationalist actors faced identical assertions by the British that industry in the colony was "unnatural." Colonial authorities claimed that India, or more precisely *Indians*, were unsuited for technology and skill intensive manufacturing activities due to their "inherent characteristics." These types

---

[43] By contrast, the Indian nationalist movement was galvanized by opposition to British merchant trade. For example, the *swadeshi* (self-reliance) movement constituted the first mass movement against colonialism organized by the elite Indian National Congress, and was organized around supporting indigenous Indian textile production and trade against the imported textiles from Lancashire. These views similarly resonated in the postwar period when India business and government actors began to negotiate with multinational firms

of race-based cultural tropes were deployed against Indians writ large, including skilled managers and engineers (Misra, 1999). However, Indian nationalism emerged in *opposition* to these colonial assertions. Indian economic nationalists believed that any observed weaknesses in Indian industry during the period of British colonialism was due to the destruction of traditional Indian industry and the deindustrialization and impoverishment of India through imperial policies of laissez-faire 'free trade', not innate differences in Indians' capacity for industry. In fact, they argued that Indian manufactures, and even Indian science, had long been *superior* to Europe's prior to the industrial revolution (Prakash, 1999).[44] In fact, Indian nationalist beliefs were explicitly formulated to challenge colonial ideas that naturalized European industrial and technological superiority, by citing India's rich manufacturing history as proof of its capacity to pursue industrial development. By contrast, in Brazil, these views – including the racialized aspects – were held by many Brazilian elites; thus, in many respects Brazilian nationalism rested on these foundations rather than in opposition to them. This had major implications for variation in the regulation of FDI at the industry level across both countries in the postwar period.[45]

Finally, as noted, the Brazilian military was a crucial source of emerging Brazilian economic nationalism as well as ideas of developmentalism that would become dominant from the 1930s onward (Sikkink, 1991). The military's concerns at this time lay with protecting Brazil's vast borders from its neighbors and developing industry that would allow Brazil to become a major power. It was much less oriented toward political, economic, or military threats from Europe. As such, economic nationalist ideas in Brazil were largely mobilized around national security concerns in resource extraction such as oil[46] and the development of basic industries such as steel. By contrast, Indian economic nationalism was motivated by achieving industrial, scientific, and technological prowess based on a collective belief that India's past artisanal skills and industrial expertise had been destroyed

---

[44] Prafulla Chandra Ray's 1903 work *A History of Hindu Chemistry from the Earliest Times to the Middle of the Sixteenth Century* is the classic nationalist text in this vein. Chandra Ray's work on indigenous Indian scientific achievements along with Romesh Chandra Dutt's two-volume *An Economic History of India* published in 1901 and 1903 provided a rich elaboration of drain theory and offered a strong empirical challenge to the classical political economy arguments about Indian backwardness.

[45] In this respect, the origins of the capitalist classes in both countries may play an important role in the different cultural schemas that emerged to shape industrial development in the twentieth century. As in India, local Brazilian capital was dominated by large diversified business groups; but unlike Indian groups, no distinction was made between the 40% of the largest "Brazilian" groups that were founded by recent European migrants. In India, such groups would be dominated by British capital and be considered "foreign," even if they had been present in India for 100 years. That is, nationality itself is socially constructed.

[46] It is worth noting that this defense objective was common across peer countries at this time, such as China, given concerns following the Japanese incursions into Manchuria in 1931 (Fertik, 2014).

by the imposition of 'free trade' policies by the British.[47] As such, Indian economic nationalism was oriented toward establishing large-scale technology-based engineering industry and ensuring domestic ownership in manufacturing industries such as automobiles more so than natural resource areas such as oil. India emerged from colonialism filled with resentment about the deindustrializing effects of extractive British imperial free trade on traditional Indian industry while their Brazilian counterparts saw foreign private capital – as well as the role of foreign powers such as the British in facilitating a free trade regime – as largely benefiting Brazil, especially relative to the constraints of Portuguese mercantilism.[48] Foreign capital facilitated the development of commodity trade, shipping infrastructure, and utilities that supported the beginning of the manufacturing industry in Brazil, while similar investments in India was seen by Indian nationalists as colonial-led extraction that promoted the *deindustrialization* of India.

These contrasting beliefs became further embedded in the Brazilian and Indian national consciousness over the first few decades of the twentieth century.[49] By the end of the Second World War, Brazil's colonial relationship with Portugal was a fading memory while India had just prevailed after decades of intense nationalist contestation with Great Britain that was organized under the anti-colonial banner of the Congress Party.[50] Independence in 1947 provided Indian economic and political actors with the long-awaited opportunity to return India to its rightful historical position as an industrial nation, while Brazilians had no such social memory of past national glories.[51]

Different social meanings were thus ascribed to industrial development in Brazil and India, generating distinct economic nationalist beliefs, with divergent industrial policy discourses and contrasting regulatory outcomes. The case selection allows for deeper consideration of the concept of nationalism itself, and how its content

---

[47] Note, however, that Nehruvian scientific socialism placed the state at the "commanding heights" of the economy with Indian private firms largely relegated to manufactured consumer goods.

[48] As indicated earlier, there is a debate in Brazilian historiography about the role of foreign capital, and indeed, one can also add the precise meaning of "foreign" in the social context of émigré post-colonial Brazil that will be explored in subsequent iterations of this research. In India, by contrast, the social meaning of "Indian" and "foreign" is much more clearly and unambiguously delineated during this period.

[49] These were embedded in the types of intersubjectively held meanings, symbols, narratives, and representations that were discussed in the previous sections.

[50] Note, however, that these views were not entirely cohesive. For example, debates raged between Nehru and Gandhi, in the period leading up to independence. Even with Nehru's victory, they returned in force from the mid-1950s onward as challenges arose to the Nehruvian consensus.

[51] The industrialization plans central to Vargas' *Estado Novo* had to overcome powerful vested interests (with the support of the military) that were content to continue with resource extraction while Indian nationalist actors, once in power after independence, faced no such resistance: there was broad-based consensus favoring self-reliant industrial development.

and meaning can vary across countries and industries depending on contingent social, political, and historical factors. These are examined in the context of the development and promotion of each country's nascent petroleum and automobile industries in the immediate post-Second World War period (1945–1964).[52]

6 The Development of the Oil Industry in Brazil and India

The introduction to this Element noted the puzzling contrast between the approach to foreign investment in the politically sensitive and economically vital petroleum industries in Brazil and India. This contrast is even more striking given that contemporary Brazil is widely recognized as a country with significant oil reserves while India is rarely mentioned among the oil producing nations of the world. Yet as noted earlier, both Brazil and India are among the top 25 countries in global proven reserves (Brazil is ranked 15th and India is ranked 24th) and, further, oil was discovered in India in the late nineteenth century, whereas Brazil had to wait almost a century longer for confirmation of the existence of serious proven reserves. Crucially for this comparative study, India had *higher* levels of proven oil reserves than Brazil for the first few decades of the postwar period, as indicated in Figure 2. What then are the sources of this striking contrast in approaches to regulating foreign capital in the oil sector?

Figure 2 Proven oil reserves (millions of barrels)

Source: *OPEC: Annual Statistical Bulletin*

---

[52] This logic of this periodization covers the initial postwar industrial development period, which almost perfectly coincide in both countries. It extends from the end of the Second World War to the death of Nehru and the authoritarian turn in India and Brazil, respectively. This represents well-established eras in both countries' industrial development history.

The Institutionalized Roots of Oil and Nationalism in Brazil and India

The fundamental root of Brazil's "natural resource" economic nationalism lay in Brazilians' deep faith that their subsoil was rich in oil and that foreign oil companies – the nefarious "trusts" – would go to great lengths to control it. This view was deeply embedded in the Brazilian public consciousness, in contrast to India, where similar beliefs about protecting oil wealth were only narrowly held among a group of technocratic elites. Despite having higher levels of proven oil reserves as well as deeply entrenched anti-colonial beliefs, the petroleum sector in India never generated the type of nationalist salience that it did in Brazil.

The first recorded oil finds in India date back to 1825 when British explorers noted petroleum seepages in Upper Assam. This finding was reinforced in 1865 with further oil shows identified by a team from the Geological Survey of India, which led to the drilling by a private British firm of Asia's first well near Digboi in 1867. The British Assam Oil Company (AOM) was formed in 1899 to exploit oil interests in the area and was acquired in 1921 by the Scottish-owned Burmah Oil Company (BOC).[53] Oil exploration thus began in India with British private interests and would remain under exclusive private foreign control for more than a decade after independence in 1947.

In Brazil anti-colonial sentiment and oil were linked from the nineteenth century when landed elites struggled to gain subsoil property rights from the imperial court. As early as 1923, when British oil companies in colonial India dominated the sector to the exclusion of American and other foreign firms, a law was proposed in Brazil under the Old Republic prohibiting concessions to foreigners, even though no oil had been discovered. The relationship between nationalism and oil in Brazil is further intertwined with the rise of Getulio Vargas. This political transformation occurred amid growing concerns in Brazil over the intentions of the "foreign trusts." Sinister plots abounded, for example, claiming that foreign oil companies were working to convince officials that the country had no oil while secretly surveying sedimentary basins and even drilling and capping wells for further use, all in order to acquire lucrative concessions at low prices. The 1934 constitution entrenched the reservation of subsoil rights in the state, granting the central government exclusive power to grant concessions for exploration and exploitation that previously lay with provincial political bosses and wealthy landlords.

---

[53] The key foreign players in India were Burmah-Shell (Burmah Oil Company and Royal Dutch Shell), Standard Vacuum (Standard Oil of NJ and Mobil Oil), and Caltex (Standard Oil of California and Texaco).

While these developments signaled the growing importance of oil among a new political elite, the politics of oil exploded in the wider Brazilian consciousness with Monteiro Lobato's 1936 publication of *O Escândalo do Petróleo* (*The Petroleum Scandal*). Lobato was an entrepreneur, and the book "was a no holds-barred attack on the government [which] according to Lobato, was engaged in trying to destroy entrepreneurial initiative and to leave the oil in the ground for the benefit of the 'trusts'" (Philips, 228). The book was immensely popular and would cast a long shadow over the industry.

The 1930s was a crucial decade in both countries that saw two key organizational developments that would shape the relationship between oil and nationalism: the rise of the military as the dominant organizational force in Brazil and the consolidation of the Indian National Congress (INC) as the chief opponent of the British and the heir apparent to India at the end of colonial rule. In Brazil, the military's influence grew over the course of this period and culminated with the suspension of the legislature and the establishment of the corporatist *Estado Novo* (New State) by Vargas in a 1937 mini-coup. Crucially, the military began to view oil as a national security issue amid concerns of a possible foreign takeover of a *future* oil industry (since at this stage there was still no evidence of oil being present in Brazil). Vargas enjoyed the support of like-minded military officials such as General Julio Cetano Horta Barbosa, who would become a central figure in the Brazilian oil industry. The new constitution went even further than its predecessor in petroleum legislation, stipulating that only Brazilians could own shares in national mining companies, banning foreign capital participation to prevent foreigners from "enriching themselves" in Brazil (Smith, 1976: 33). Decree Law 366 declared all yet-to-be discovered oilfields as Federal property while Decree Law 395 established national petroleum supply as a public utility, nationalized the refining industry, and created the National Petroleum Council (CNP) to control the industry with Horta Barbosa at its helm.

These deepening Brazilian views were influenced by regional developments. Mexico expropriated its entire petroleum industry in March 1938 amid long-standing difficulties regulating foreign firm participation in what was already a profitable industry. The Argentinian *Yacimientos Petrolíferos Fiscales* (YPF) also served as a model of a state-owned firm, though it was created *after* Argentina found oil while the CNP was created *before* there was any evidence of petroleum deposits. However, on January 21, 1939, oil was struck in the Bahia Recôncavo, confirming what "every Brazilian in his heart of hearts had always believed" (Smith, 1976: 37). Monteiro Lobato was vindicated in telling the Brazilian public to believe in oil wealth, but also had been legislated out of the industry along with other private companies.

The Brazilian National Petroleum Council and the Second World War

Horta Barbosa became a key figure in efforts to eliminate competition with the CNP. Barbosa was a savvy choice by Vargas: He saw oil as providing security from foreigners in both peace and war and was committed to a corporatist mode of oil development. Vargas gave him a free hand, while Barbosa helped ensure military support to Vargas' presidency. While Barbosa was against foreign ownership in the industry, he was not against external assistance and began by seeking exploration machinery from the United States along with US technicians to train Brazilians. He was aided by two decrees that unified tariffs under CNP control and established a national refinery that would ensure potentially high profits would be used in the nation's interests to promote the fledgling industry by financing exploration rather than going to private benefit. Barbosa and others feared that private capital could facilitate the entry of foreign monopolies and so needed a source of revenue. Self-financing oil efforts were thus extremely valuable.

Despite these efforts, the CNP had a miniscule budget of only US$250,000 in 1939, which grew to a mere US$1.5 million in 1940–1943. This was insufficient for funding exploration, and in 1940, a foreign group – believed to be Standard Oil of New Jersey operating through its local subsidiary – expressed interest in joint exploration through a mixed state–private company, offering to cover exploration and production costs in exchange for a percentage of crude with distribution rights. Despite the CNP's dire lack of funds, this prospect alarmed Barbosa, who sent a memo to Army Chief of Staff General Goés Monteiro citing the Constitution and Decree-Law 395. Barbosa also highlighted the Venezuelan example, claiming that once entrenched, foreign companies exerted a "colonial" degree of control "over the complete economic life of the nation, to the extent of fixing the exchange rate of its currency" (Smith, 1976: 41). Nevertheless, Cabinet ignored Barbosa's position and approved the venture almost unanimously. Barbosa offered his resignation, but Vargas assured him that it would not go through, and indeed it quietly died. This signaled the emerging political conflict between competing groups advocating liberal and restrictive positions in the oil arena.

By this time, the Second World War was raging and wartime shortages led to fuel rationing as tankers were diverted to war theatres. Standard Oil Company of Brazil made another offer to Vargas that included a request for a constitutional amendment to guarantee profits. This was the type of strong-armed strategy that the oil majors would successfully attempt in India. But in Brazil, the cabinet was split. Barbosa again objected on the basis of sovereignty and national security, framing the "trusts" as agents of US foreign policy. Minister of War General Gaspar Dutra also urged rejection. Vargas again complied and tabled the proposal.

In delineating the battle lines between these competing groups, it is important to note that Vargas was not completely anti-FDI. In fact, he preferred a mixed arrangement between the public and private (including foreign) sector to launch the oil industry, much as he had sought in the steel industry with Volta Redonda. However, the army was behind Horta Barbosa's corporatist solutions and Vargas was unwilling to challenge them. In the meantime, Brazil continued to refuse foreign assistance even while exploration was faring poorly and the fuel crisis grew. The country was subject to heavy rationing as private owners parked cars and factories shut down for lack of fuel oil. Even the CNP faced parts shortages that shut down exploration in all but the Recôncavo, while national production was mere 1% of demand at 300 barrels per day. To cap off the wartime crisis, Horta Barbosa himself suddenly resigned from the CNP in August 1943.

Failed Attempts at a Liberal Postwar Turn in Brazil

The immediate postwar period saw deepening of divisions between liberal and restrictive approaches to foreign capital. Army Colonel João Carlos Barreto took over the CNP with a focus on rapid oil development that included foreign participation. Vargas appeared to concur with Barreto and attempted to push a new law that would allow 50% foreign participation in exploration. The law contradicted the constitution and so failed but served as another indication of Vargas' moderate position. More broadly, a growing liberal turn among the Brazilian middle classes highlighted contradictions between the authoritarian *Estado Novo* and Brazil's wartime cooperation with the anti-fascist Allies. Vargas' position was untenable, and he ultimately resigned, with General Eurico Dutra elected president in 1946.

Dutra also adopted an increasingly liberal view toward oil. Fascism and "perverse" nationalism were deemed "out of fashion," and "Horta Barbosa's rigid nationalist stance was as anachronistic as *Estado Novo*" (Smith, 1976). Instead, an "open" oil policy was promoted, with the only restriction being that companies should be formed in Brazil, no matter nationality of share ownership. This "liberal" approach was at odds with the earlier attitude toward oil as well as with the return to nationalist backlash that was to come; however, it was consistent with the view that would prevail in the Brazilian auto sector in the 1950s. The liberal push continued with General Juarez Távora campaigning to open petroleum to both private domestic *and* foreign capital as a means of development. Having observed the effect of war on Brazil's petroleum supplies and the importance of oil in the European theatre, Távora believed national security intrinsically rested on solving the "petroleum problem." However, to resolve the issue he claimed Brazil shouldn't adopt a "pseudo-nationalist" policy (Smith, 1976: 53) illustrating the diversity of views that can be considered "nationalist" (Helleiner, 2002).

Távora's statements prompted Horta Barbosa to go on the offensive. Barbosa claimed that petroleum fundamentally belonged to the nation, citing examples of Mexico and Argentina where state ownership supported national goals, versus Venezuela and Paraguay where it benefited wealthy individuals and the foreign "trusts." For Barbosa, conflicts between the "trusts" and the state were inevitable. Most importantly, this battle between Barbosa and Távora reflected an emerging split within the military, as both embarked on public campaigns advocating their competing positions. Távora argued for maintaining the US-Brazilian alliance established during the war, positing oil as a strategic asset that could only be developed through FDI. Barbosa countered with the state enterprise option by arguing that if the United States wanted Brazil to develop oil, it should provide loans to do so. Barbosa claimed that financing exploration through domestic refineries was a superior development strategy. Crucially, his claims were also couched in national security terms:

> In principle, I am not sympathetic to the ideas of an industrializing state. However, I am a firm defender of it in matters of energy and, particularly, of petroleum ... although the crude oil market is competitive, refining is essentially monopolistic and is controlled either by the trusts or the state ... Exploration, development and refining are parts of a whole, which is capable of ensuring political and economic power ... It is not permissable to give outsiders the responsibility for an activity which is tied [to] national security. (Philips, 234)

Barbosa's view resonated with the military and was promoted by a coterie of officers who hired a public relations agency and distributed 3,000 letters on Military Club letterhead to key recipients deemed capable of influencing public opinion. By the end of 1948, the army was "overwhelmingly pro-Horta" (Philips, 234). Unlike India, where differences on oil were resolved at the elite level, the Brazilian debate deepened as it shifted to the public domain. Street protests erupted around the central rallying cry: *O petróleo é nosso* (the oil is ours) inspired by Barbosa's speeches. The Communist Party as well as student activists who expected industrial jobs created by the shift in industrial structure under the *Estado Novo* and who feared foreign industrial control vigorously pursued these protests.[54] Standard Oil Company of Brazil launched a vigorous US$140,000

---

[54] It is crucial to note that each of these groups rationalized their positions by deploying different strands of nationalism: one favoring what Thomas Skidmore (1969, 1988) and others have called developmentalist nationalism that favored mixed companies under state control with the other

advertising campaign across 30 newspapers, aiming to convince the Brazilian public that, as a foreign oil company, they had the essential know-how to develop the complex petroleum industry, but to no avail (Time Magazine, 1949). The liberal petroleum bill floundered and ultimately failed. The Horta Barbosa faction within the military was victorious. *O petróleo é nosso* won the day.

Independence in India and the New Oil Question

The Indian National Congress (INC) assumed control of newly independent India in a series of steps as the British prepared to depart their soon-to-be former colony. By the 1940s the INC was largely united under Nehru in its anti-imperial sentiment, but it was politically heterogeneous in every other respect, comprising moderates, liberals, socialists, and conservatives. The entire ideological continuum was represented in its ranks. Nehru himself was a statist developmentalist, committed to the pursuit of modern large-scale industry under state control where possible, but cognizant of the need for foreign technology to ensure industrial success. Nehru also recognized the diversity of perspectives within his party and proceeded cautiously and democratically in determining the economic policies that newly independent India would pursue.

The most important organ of economic policy formulation was the National Planning Committee, which first convened in 1938, the last few years of colonial rule. The committee identified power and fuel as a key area and recommended efforts in search of petroleum resources. The committee's activities lay dormant during the war when Nehru and others were imprisoned but regained steam in 1945. The question of foreign investment was central with the general view being that private foreign capital had dominated India throughout the late colonial period and thus a wary approach was warranted. Crucially, India's oil supply at this time was completely dominated by foreign oil majors, the same "trusts" that Brazilians feared and which controlled world oil supply. Oil import prices were completely determined by the Anglo-American firms, a situation that had served British colonial interests well but was problematic for the anti-imperial Congress Party. In July 1947, the Interim Government contacted the three companies with monopoly distribution rights – Burmah Shell, Standard Vacuum, and Caltex – about the feasibility of establishing oil refineries and pursuing exploration in India. These firms indicated little interest in exploration in India, given their cheap and seemingly secure supplies from the Gulf coupled with India's unknown petroleum geology outside of Assam, which, as in Brazil, was (wrongly) assumed

---

strand claiming that Brazil was in a subordinate position vis-à-vis foreign capital and a (comprador) domestic bourgeois that sought to keep Brazil in a colonial position. For this group, total state control was necessary to prevent this neocolonial subordination.

to be unfavorable. Instead, they demanded guarantees against expropriation of exploration assets and refineries. These assurances were highly unusual at the time. Yet, despite similarities in their situations and in stark contrast to Brazil, the Indian Cabinet accepted these stringent terms.[55]

The situation changed radically in 1951 with the nationalization of the Anglo-Iranian Oil Company by revolutionary Prime Minister Dr. Mohammed Mossadeq. This prompted a wave of expropriations in Libya, Iraq, and across the Middle East and North Africa as newly independent governments rebelled against the exploitative royalties these companies charged. These spread to countries in other regions from Asia (Burma in 1962; Indonesia in 1963) to Latin America (Argentina in 1963; Peru in 1968). As this period progressed there were forty-three cases of nationalizations in the oil sector in twenty-four countries over twenty-one years (Ostrovski, 2023).

International law may have also come to play a role with the advancement of the concept of permanent sovereignty over natural resources by UN delegates from Bolivia, Iran, and Mexico in 1952, and anticolonial elites across the decolonizing world began to see the potential of international legal rules for the projects of securing economic sovereignty through the process of "world-making" (Ostrovski, 2023; see also Getachew, 2019). Foreign interest in exploration and especially refining in India suddenly began to grow as India was seen as a potential safe haven. Burmah Shell, Stanvac, and Caltex all agreed to set up refineries in India for a total investment of US$120 million, albeit with even more stringent demands. This spate of nationalizations could be interpreted as reflecting the erosion of the structural power of the oil majors, their diminishing control over the global industry, and the extent to which initial bargains had "obsolesced." Yet the Indian government nevertheless continued to accept the oil majors' unfavorable terms.

The Return of Vargas and the Formation of Petrobrás

By the late 1940s Vargas was plotting a return to politics with the formation of the Brazilian Labor Party (PTB). His campaign was organized around twin "ideologies" of *desenvolvimentismo* and *trabalhismo* (developmentalism and laborism), and signaled restrictions on foreign capital in oil if he returned to office while hedging against total exclusion.[56] Vargas won the 1951 election by

---

[55] The terms were as follows: (1) Government would not nationalize for thirty years; (2) crude imports would remain with the foreign oil companies for thirty years; and (3) distribution of refined products would also remain with the foreign oil companies for thirty years (Kaul, 1991: 3).

[56] "Let us speak clearly: that which is indispensable to national defense, which constitutes the basis of our sovereignty, may not be handed over to foreign interests; it must be exploited by Brazilians through organizations predominantly Brazilian, and, if possible, with a high percentage of state

striking political deals with the old bosses and sought a compromise on oil, which he saw as a central plank in major new development plans involving both private and public sectors. However, Vargas severely underestimated the power of *O petróleo é nosso*.

In December 1951, Vargas proposed Law 2004 that would create *Petróleo Brasileiro Sociedade Anônima (Petrobrás)*. The firm would monopolize the industry, except distribution, where private domestic and foreign actors would be allowed to operate. Petrobrás would be financed by domestic capital through an initial US$200 million subscription by the state coupled with public shareholding and taxes. The political debate again reflected the divide between those advocating for a degree of private participation and those who pushed for full state control. Opponents, including voices from within Vargas' PTB, advanced a "Trojan horse" argument that the Vargas bill would facilitate opportunities for foreign trusts, since subsidiaries of firms such as Standard Oil could purchase shares and, in principle, acquire sufficient ownership share to seize managerial control. Instead, they wanted a bill that would guarantee full state control. Public sentiment in favor of state control was powerful at this time and even the anti-Vargas UDN adopted a state monopoly view, perhaps recognizing the power of *O petróleo é nosso* (Smith, 1976: 85).

Yet the statist solution was not without challenges as fiscal concerns continued to loom large in Brazil. Foreign exchange needs were rising with the growing petroleum import bill, and Brazil was paying US$200 million per year in hard currency for oil. Despite its industrialization efforts, Brazil remained heavily reliant on coffee, which accounted for 70% of hard currency earnings, while other Brazilian exports were faring poorly. Brazil was in a near-identical position with India, which was similarly reliant on traditional exports of tea, cotton, and jute. However, those in favor of the statist solution downplayed the costs of creating a state oil industry while citing the extensive savings that the industry would create. That is, Brazilian fiscal concerns were used to *rationalize* oil investments, while in India they were used to *preclude* state investment, with Nehru's own spending preferences remaining with heavy engineering industry.

The Petrobrás bill hit the Senate in October 1952, pitting the *entreguistas* (sellouts) versus nationalists. The former claimed that "Our petroleum will remain buried eternally if we do not have foreign assistance," while the latter argued that "It's better that it remain buried for the glory of future generations, than it be handed over to the exploitation of the international trusts" (Smith, 1976: 92). At the same time, other voices questioned the widespread assumption

---

participation, avoiding in this way surreptitious penetration by threatening monopolies" (Cited in Smith, 1976: 74).

that the Brazil had vast oil resources, which was still completely unproven. However, these voices were dismissed as representing devious efforts of the "trusts" seeking foreign exploration. The debate continued for months, but ultimately the vote was 3–1 in favor of the statist solution. On October 3, 1953, Vargas signed Law 2004 creating Petrobrás, which was the product of public sentiment and political debates rather than Vargas' own position.

Economic liberals, including many within the anti-Vargas factions in the military such as General Juarez Távora, remained against Petrobrás and the exclusion of foreign capital. Petrobrás was closely identified with Vargas, even though he was never in favor of total foreign exclusion, preferring a balanced solution as with his efforts in launching the steel industry. Nevertheless, an anti-foreign nationalist Petrobrás became synonymous with Vargas. This perception was cemented when, facing growing political turmoil, Vargas committed suicide on August 24, 1954, leaving a note famously blaming "a subterranean campaign of international groups joined with national groups" that were working against him, including attempting to block initiatives such as Petrobrás. The claims of the suicide note played into decades-old public sentiment about *still* yet-to-be-discovered Brazilian oil wealth and the nefarious foreign forces represented by the *entreguistas* at home and the "trusts" abroad. Crucially, it also resonated with other nationalist leaders outside of Brazil who were also struggling with the question of foreign firm participation in oil, including Jawaharlal Nehru in India.

Nationalism and Conflict over Petrobrás

Petrobrás was formally launched on January 1, 1954, with Army Colonel Juracy Magalhães as its first President.[57] Magalhães was pragmatic about foreign assistance to support the nascent state-owned firm, and Law 2004 allowed foreign technical assistance. Magalhães brought in a group of foreign technicians, most notably the American Walter Link, who was to become a major divisive figure. Link was the former chief exploration geologist for Standard Oil of New Jersey and was considered one of the leading petroleum geologists in the world. He was hired to lead the Exploration Department (DEPEX). In keeping with this approach, the CNP opened bids for Brazilian crude oil supply and by 1955 Petrobrás had signed US$300 million worth of contracts with foreign entities.

---

[57] On April 2, 1954, all CNP assets were turned over to Petrobrás. These assets were valued at US$165 million and included production fields, a refinery, twenty-two tankers, and drilling equipment. Crude production at this stage was 2,500bpd, and the CNP had drilled a total of 4,040 wells, 367 of which were in Bahia and 244 of which had yielded oil, all in Bahia.

The nationalist debate on oil and Petrobrás persisted after Vargas' death. New President Café Filho was open to foreign capital, as was the liberal Finance Minister Eugenio Gudin, who had held many executive positions with MNCs and was seen as an arch-*entreguista*. However, by this stage the military had closed ranks and even General Távora declared a change of heart. Vargas' suicide was a powerful determining factor, ensuring widespread military support for Petrobrás and preventing the Café Filho administration from diverting from the nationalistic course upon which Brazil had embarked.

The later rise of Juescilino Kubitschek to the Presidency in 1956 further ensured the continuation of nationalist rhetoric. Kubitschek won the election with Vargas' base of old party bosses and urban labor. The Kubitschek administration was committed to "developmentalist nationalism" and energy was seen as a bottleneck to growth, thus ensuring the oil question remained at the center of Brazilian politics.[58] Kubitschek also faced a threat from War Minister General Henrique Teixeira Lott, who told him "I regret having to say to your Excellency that, should the Petrobrás law be modified, the Army will find itself wondering whether to withdraw completely its support from the government."

Kubitschek also began explicitly using Petrobrás for political purposes in 1957, claiming, like Vargas, that there was a campaign against him which aimed "the weakening of the nationalistic oil policy" and "conspire[d] against the economic development of Brazil." The debate persisted with liberal economist Roberto Campos (who was sometimes sarcastically referred to as "Bob Fields") penning an early 1957 article entitled "The Three Fallacies about Present-Day Brazil" attacking the idea of state monopoly in Law 2004. Campos suggested keeping Petrobrás, but he preferred cooperation with foreign firms to ease foreign exchange pressures and high exploration costs (US$300 million by 1960). Campos decried "romantic nationalism" and wanted to trade "units of vanity" for "units of wealth." He acknowledged the possibility of long-term savings but at very high short-term cost. Helio Beltrao countered in the publication *Ultima Hora* that the interests of Brazil and the trusts do not intersect. Given overproduction at the time, trusts had no incentive to develop Brazilian fields in short term, especially since Brazil's oil import bill was US$250 million per year. This is the same argument that would be deployed in India.

By this time, Petrobrás was exceeding production targets, having attained its 1960 goal of 40,000 barrels/day (up from 6,500 when Kubitschek took office). However, while production had increased, new exploration was not going well. In

---

[58] The centerpiece of Kubitschek's developmentalist vision was the construction of the new capital of Brasilia deep in the Amazon, as well as state direction and import substitution, of which the automobile industry would be the key, albeit with foreign capital taking the lead. This is further discussed in the section of the development of the Brazilian auto industry.

1960, Walter Link co-authored a report that offered a pessimistic view of Amazonian fields. The report suggested Brazil secure external crude sources and pursue offshore exploration. The report was confidential but was leaked, generating nationalist reaction claiming Link was a "tool of imperialists" who had sabotaged exploration efforts. Though the American Link was part of a fourteen-person team that included six Brazilian geologists, critics began referring to "Linkism" as a defeatist tendency, and even the president of Petrobrás dismissed the report as the work of agents of "the trusts." The view was still that Petrobrás was less trying to discover oil rather than prove its existence.

The politicization of Petrobrás continued in the 1960–1964 period, with the Link report coupled with accusations of internal mismanagement. The Chamber of Deputies convened an inquiry in March 1961 over the "Link Report" and ultimately characterized it as an *entreguista* attack on Petrobrás. The critical view was that the Link Report was a product of Standard Oil's methods, which were to choose only best fields and abandon those that were deemed mediocre from a commercial perspective, an approach that could not be adopted in Brazil. Petrobrás thus continued scattered efforts across the Brazilian sedimentary basin with every oil show used by the PR department to prove Link wrong.

The crisis deepened with reports that Petrobrás was in a precarious financial position. The firm became deeply embroiled in broader political divisions that were emerging in Brazil, reflected in a series of articles published in *Ultima Hora* by leading army officers with titles like "Without the State Petroleum Monopoly, We Will Not Arrive at Economic Emancipation!" (General Barbosa), "Defence of the State Monopoly is a Patriotic Duty of All Brazilians" (General Lott), and "The Armed Forces Defend the State Petroleum Monopoly" (General Alves, leader of the First Army).

By 1960, Brazil was mired in political crisis with the military threatening to take over. Recently installed leftist President João Goulart was seen as politically weak and by 1963 was under severe political pressure amid open talks of coups. Petrobrás was also faring poorly financially, and nationalists were clamoring for expropriation of private refineries, with workers striking in favor. Finally, amid the debates around Petrobrás' future, in August 1963 Petrobrás announced that two Soviet technicians claimed that Brazil possessed commercially viable petroleum in great quantities and advised intensification of drilling. Newspaper reports claimed Brazil could quadruple production in five years. The "Russian Report" was seen as complete refutation of the pessimistic "Link Report," and the Russians were seen as potentially "ending the domain of American Saboteurs within Petrobrás." In reality, the Russians were also critical of Petrobrás, noting that its drilling techniques were substandard, its production methods weak, and its planning processes bureaucratized and overly focused on short- rather than long-term gains. In the wake of this announcement, the 1964 coup became a watershed for Petrobrás, as the new authoritarian military government insulated the company from the broad political debates within which it had become embedded and placed it on a new path where it was dominated by technocrats and refocused on the goals of exploration and finding Brazil's oil wealth, a task it would continue for the next three decades before finally achieving major offshore finds in the 1990s and 2000s (with then-President Lula da Silva dubbing the 2007 find the *bilhete premiado* or "winning ticket").

Foreign Firms and Exploration in India

While national security concerns loomed large in Brazil's natural resource–oriented economic nationalism, India's relative ambivalence toward multinational corporations in petroleum is puzzling, not only given its more recent and harsh colonial experience, but also in terms of its own security woes. Brazil's twentieth-century security worries were somewhat abstract given that it faced no serious threats from its neighbors or other adversaries further afield. Much of the angst was generated by military officers' participation in the European front during the Second World War. India, by contrast, faced direct threats that ultimately manifested in multiple skirmishes and three all-out wars with China and Pakistan in the first two decades of independence. The relationship between oil and national security in India was exemplified by the fact that some of its most promising oil-bearing structures were shared with Pakistan, extending across both countries with little regard for their politically determined borders or Cold War alliances.

The US firm Standard Vacuum (a subsidiary of Standard Oil of New Jersey, the American oil company from which Walter Link came) was surveying the Bengal Basin, and by 1952 it became clear that oil might be present in a geological structure that extended across India and East Pakistan (now Bangladesh). The question became which side would Standard Vacuum drill on. The issue was deeply entrenched in emerging Cold War tensions. Pakistan had established itself as a clear US ally, while India sought to maintain a nonaligned posture but was also friendly with the Soviet Union. Standard Vacuum's surveying activities were also occurring a few short years after the bloody experience of Partition and threatened to increase tensions between the two countries. The contrast with Brazil is striking. While Vargas and the military were establishing a state-owned monopoly to exclusively pursue exploration under the aegis of anti-imperialism and national security, India faced real concerns of neo-imperialism as well as direct security threats, yet Nehru and the Congress eschewed the option of forming a fully owned Indian concern and continued to negotiate an agreement with Standard Vacuum. This was ultimately deemed to be a gift to Standard Vacuum. Not only did the agreement seem to be at odds with the Industrial Policy Resolution of 1948, but it also allowed a foreign firm full control over the pace and extent of exploration efforts, which it pursued "with leisure" (Kaul, 1991: 35–37).

The Standard Vacuum experience sparked tensions within the Indian bureaucracy, particularly between the liberal Dr. S.S. Bhatnagar of the Ministry of Natural Resources and Scientific Research, who favored extensive engagement with the oil majors, and K.D. Malaviya, then Parliamentary Secretary, who advocated strongly for a restrictive approach, first with his colleagues within the Ministry, and then directly with Nehru himself. While Bhatnagar and other liberals within the Congress Party sought to entrust foreign firms with oil prospecting in India, Malaviya began to campaign for Indian solutions involving the state and domestic private capital. He pushed strongly for the creation of an Oil and Natural Gas Division within the ministry that would be responsible for oil exploration. This debate closely mirrored Brazil's. And indeed, the Latin American experience loomed large, as Bhatnagar favorably cited the examples of partnerships with foreign firms in Venezuela as models for India. Malaviya, by contrast, adopted a position that was similar to Barbosa by warning of the dangers of ceding control of exploration to foreign firms that had interests that diverged significantly from India's.

Nehru himself appeared uncertain about the direction India should take. On one hand, he was wary of the neo-imperial threat posed by the oil majors and was troubled by Vargas' suicide. On the other hand, he was apprehensive of the reaction of liberals in the Finance Ministry to the hefty cost of "speculative" oil exploration. These concerns were deepened by the fact that, like Brazil, India lacked technical skills and know-how in the area, making the decision even more difficult. Foreign experts offered mixed opinions about the prospects for commercial discoveries in India and ultimately efforts to secure financial assistance through President Truman's Point Four Program failed, though, as in Brazil, this led India to the Soviet Union.

Malaviya achieved a breakthrough with Soviet and Romanian assistance, and the death of Bhatnagar opened the way for the creation of the Oil and Natural Gas Commission. However, in contrast to Petrobrás, the ONGC had limited resources and an unclear mandate. More fundamentally, its rise and fall reflected the relative ambivalence in India toward establishing domestic ownership and control of the oil industry. Negotiations with the Assam Oil Company and the Burmah Oil Company resulted in a jointly owned entity, Oil India Limited (OIL), that would engage in refining activities. However, OIL and the ONGC were mixed successes. OIL represented efforts by the Indian government to establish control over refining and, hence, domestic fuel prices. Yet what ensued was years of battles over pricing with foreign firms who continued to maintain substantial, though not completely monopolistic, positions in the industry. Meanwhile, ONGC found success in exploration in the late 1950s, notably in a region (Gujarat) where foreign firms had expressed pessimism. This experience was much like Petrobrás and similarly justified Malaviya's efforts and the investments in ONGC. However, unlike Petrobrás, this did not result in exclusive powers being conferred to ONGC. Instead, foreign firms retained their central role in exploration throughout the 1960s. The maintenance of dominant positions in Indian petroleum industry not only stands in contrast to the Brazilian experience, but also with the Indian experience in the auto industry where its "manufacturing"-oriented economic nationalism helped secure dominant positions for private Indian firms while relegating foreign partners to subordinate positions, the precise opposite from what would unfold in Brazil, as this Element will now show.

7 The Development of the Auto Industry in India and Brazil

Launching the Indian Auto Industry

Serious plans for an Indian automobile industry emerged in the early 1930s while the colony was still under British control. The idea was initially championed by Sir M. Visvesvaraya, a civil engineer and civil servant who was a member of the National Planning Commission and an influential voice in elite discussions around the development of Indian industry. Visvesvaraya had traveled to Japan in 1898 where he witnessed the industrialization efforts that were taking place under the direction of the Japanese state during the Meiji Revolution. His experience ingrained in him the belief that "industrial life ... connotes production, wealth, power and modernity."[59] Four decades later Visvesvaraya made his views on the importance of the auto industry clear in a 1938 editorial in the Indian journal *Science and Culture*: " ... if we take the motor car industry as an index of civilized existence, the USA stands easily first, with over 30 million cars in use; about one man in 5 possesses a car, i.e. every family possesses a car ... in India, there is one car for every 2,300 persons. This figure gives an appalling picture of the low index of civilized life in India" (Zachariah, 2005: 238). This view of India's "backwardness" and the perception of autos as the path to modernity epitomized the type of statist developmentalism that was becoming dominant among Congress Party elites, and these ideas in turn shaped postindependence policy approaches to developing the industry.

Additionally, and in contrast to Brazil, many Indian industrialists shared this belief in the central role of the auto industry, not only for national development

---

[59] *Science and Culture*, cited in Zachariah (2005: 238).

but also for the growth of their emerging corporate empires. Visvesvaraya developed a detailed proposal for the development of an Indian auto manufacturing facility with annual production of 10,000 cars and 5,000 trucks. He proposed the flotation of a joint stock company named Indian Motors Ltd. in 1936 involving major Indian business actors such as Indian shipping magnate and staunch economic nationalist Walchand Hirachand, as well as G.D. Birla, J. R.D. Tata, and Purshotamdas Thakurdas, among others. As was the case in Brazil, none of these business actors had any experience with an industry as complex as integrated automobile production, so there was early recognition that foreign firm participation would be necessary in order to access vehicle design and production technology, as well as for technical assistance to set up the manufacturing facilities. However, consistent with India's manufacturing nationalism, and in stark contrast to Brazil, this participation would not be on a 50–50 basis, as it was feared this would lead to Indians losing managerial control to foreigners. This was a clear legacy of emerging Indian capitalists' negative experiences with the British managing agencies, under whom they were consigned to subordinate positions by British colonial economic policies (Jackson, 2025). Instead, the plan called for a lump sum payment to launch the factory and transfer technical management from foreign to local engineers over a 12- to 18-month period with fixed-term per-unit royalty payments for technology.

The local Indian Motors consortium fell apart as G.D. Birla and others decided to enter the industry on their own. However, Walchand Hirachand continued to pursue the Visvesvaraya plan and entered into negotiations with Henry Ford himself in Michigan in July 1939. The Hirachand team's demands were significant: They wanted access to all new Ford designs, a monopoly in South Asia, support with acquisition of capital equipment, worker training, and factory design and construction. In return, Ford insisted on receiving a 51% share of the venture. This was steadfastly refused by Hirachand. Instead, he offered a fixed royalty and maximum US$500,000 share sale, albeit with no voting rights and stringent transfer restrictions. This included a right of first refusal and a proviso that shares could only be sold to another Indian company. Fascinatingly, Hirachand preferred to have a local rival buy in to his firm than a foreign company.

The Ford negotiations ultimately failed, but Hirachand was undeterred. He managed to strike a similar deal with Chrysler for the manufacture of Chrysler, Dodge, and Plymouth passenger cars and trucks purely on the basis of royalty payments with no share ownership or board representation by the US firm. Chrysler accepted and the new firm, Premier Automobiles, was launched in 1944 with an aggressive plan of phased indigenization with Chrysler's support. Hirachand later entered into a similar agreement with the Italian firm Fiat, resulting in Premier producing a local version of the Fiat Padmini, which for the next few decades became the ubiquitous taxi in Bombay.

G.D. Birla remained keen to enter into automobile production and eventually struck two separate deals, one with the US firm Studebaker for the manufacture of light commercial vehicles (pickup trucks), and the other with Lord Nuffield, head of the UK-based Morris Motors Ltd., to assemble passenger cars. Nationalist pride was explicit as Birla's auto firm was named Hindustan Motors Ltd. This was not just symbolic. In the case of the latter arrangement, Morris "was to have no financial interest direct or indirect in the capital of this company and have nothing to do with its management or control." The Managing Director of Morris himself further added: "The basis of this cooperative effort is that if there is going to be an Indian car manufactured by Indians for the Indian market and if the finance is provided from Indian sources the administrative control of the project should be vested in Indian hands."[60] Nevertheless, Birla launched the firm with the intention of fully indigenizing production of the Morris Ten. The car was sold in India under the name Ambassador, and it quickly became the vehicle of choice for Indian government officials and politicians, a status it retained for decades. The iconic Ambassador is synonymous with postwar Indian manufacturing industry. It would become a potent symbol of both the achievements and pitfalls of the Indian ISI period.

Other Indian business houses followed suit. The Tata Group formed a 70–30 share partnership with Daimler in the early 1950s, and quickly became the leading manufacturer of large trucks. Mahindra and Mahindra similarly partnered with the Willys-Overland Motors to assemble jeeps, becoming a major supplier to the Indian police and military, and with Ford for the manufacture of tractors, a partnership that benefited significantly when the Green Revolution was launched in the 1960s. These two partnerships are useful to note as the Tata–Daimler relationship continued until well into the 1990s after liberalization was launched, when Tata entered passenger car manufacturing on its own after the industry was delicensed. Similarly, Ford was the multinational partner that Mahindra turned to when they decided to reenter sports utility production in the late 1990s. Ford provided some assistance in the production of the wildly successful Mahindra Scorpio, which cemented the firm's transformation from a tractor manufacturer to a full-fledged automobile producer. Thus, as Table 2 indicates, Indian capital came to dominate the newly founded auto industry with foreign firms in minority share positions or acting mainly as technology suppliers.

---

[60] In fact, other sources suggested that Morris was to receive 25–30% of the shares. However, majority ownership and managerial control remained firmly in Birla's hands (Mukherjee, 2002: 378). Birla also struck a deal with Studebaker for the manufacture of light commercial vehicles (pickup trucks) where his firm Hindustan Motors similarly held managerial control.

Table 2 Indian passenger and vehicle market share

Indian passenger and utility vehicle market share, 1955–2001 (%)	1955	1960	1970	1980	1990
Hindustan Motors (Birla Group with Morris, UK)	38	38	51	48	12
Premier (PAL; Hirachand Group, with Chrysler and Fiat)	28	27	27	19	20
SMP (Birla Group with GM)	12	14	1	0	0
Mahindra and Mahindra (with Ford, Willys, Chrysler)	22	22	21	33	15
Maruti Udyog (with Suzuki)	–	–	–	–	53

Source: *D'Costa (Ec Nationalism in Motion, 2006) Table 2 * Excludes commercial vehicles, e.g. Tata's Telco with Mercedes, Birla's Hindustan Motors with Studebaker, Ford with Amalgamations and Ashok Leyland*

Launching the Brazilian Auto Industry

The pattern of development and the role of foreign capital in Brazil could hardly be more different. Initial plans for an automobile industry in Brazil were laid in the late 1940s and early 1950s, when Admiral Lúcio Meira directed the sub-commission on motor vehicle production under Vargas' 1951–1954 administration. Meira's interest in autos had a similar genesis to Visvesvaraya's. Meira's belief in the powerful developmental role of the auto industry was sparked during his first trip to the United States in 1930, where he gained an understanding of the central position the auto industry held in the vibrant and powerful US economy. Meira "learned that one in eight American jobs was connected to auto production," and concluded that "As in the highly industrialized countries, the automotive industry in Brazil is becoming and will be without doubt the leading sector of the entire economy, by force of its magnitude, complexity, and dynamism" (Shapiro, 1994: 39).

Though the automobile production plan that the Meira subcommission developed was not adopted by the Vargas administration, Meira later shared the proposal with soon-to-be President Juscelino Kubitschek when the two met during a campaign visit to Bahia in 1955. Meira put forward a convincing argument for the inclusion of auto production in Kubitschek's proposed state-sponsored industrialization program, the Target Plan of National Development. The plan was being promoted through the modernist motto *Fifty Years of Progress in Five*, which aptly captured the widely held optimism and developmental aspirations of the postwar era. Meira's auto proposal had powerful appeal. Kubitschek needed a modern industry that would capture the imagination of the aspirational Brazilian public. On the other hand, the successful development of highway infrastructure had become a public sign of the state's capacity for competent governance, and the Brazilian middle classes that were a key part of Kubitschek's political constituency were clamoring for autos. Kubitschek immediately tested the idea at a political rally later that very same afternoon, promising to launch the production of what he termed as a "national car." The proposal garnered an enthusiastic response, and, with Kubitschek's electoral victory in 1956, Meira was named Minister of Transportation and Public Works and charged with developing the plans for launching an auto manufacturing industry (Shapiro, 1994: 28).

From the outset, the Brazilian auto industry was seen as a crucial means of attracting foreign capital and technology and generating industrial development by acting as the centerpiece of an integrated industrial structure.[61] This view arose from policymakers' beliefs in emerging economic development theories associated with Albert Hirschman (1958) and others predicated on the existence of extensive backward and forward linkages between industries and sectors across the economy. These theories were bolstered by the development of analytic tools such as input and output matrices that allowed economic planners to quantitatively model economic relationships across the industrial sector and the wider macroeconomy.[62] These models quantified the effects of industrial linkages and rationalized Brazil's entry into the production of high-technology consumer goods. Planners expected that autos would facilitate the development of complementary industries, and further support emerged from the recognition of common patterns of sectoral interdependence in other developing and industrialized economies. "Targeting high-linkage industries became the logical development strategy" (Shapiro, 1994: 40).[63] Crucially, while the developmental power of autos was clear, concerns with foreign *ownership* and *control* that dominated the oil industry did not have the same salience in the automobile industry. Autos were not seen as an avenue through which to enable the development of a domestically-owned industry or a Brazilian industrialist class.

---

[61] Brazilian policymakers had been concerned about the explosion of imports of automotive products, from US$20 million to $276 million, before falling to US$52 million in 1955 as the auto program got going.

[62] Cf. Chenery et al., 1953. This new method of economic planning was spearheaded in India by the statistician PC Mahalanobis, and was a powerful tool in the creation of India's five year plans.

[63] Brazilian technocrat Roberto Campos (pejoratively known among his detractors as "Bob Fields" for his for his liberal, pro-American positions) authored a section of the *Report of the Joint Brazil-United States Economic Development Commission* that stated: "Brazil ... offered striking evidence of the interrelationships of an economy and how accelerated growth in one sector is often the precondition for faster growth in other sectors" (Chenery et al., 1953, p. 14, cited in Sikkink 1991: 65).

FDI in the Brazilian Auto Industry

The Vargas subcommission and the subsequent Executive Group for the Auto Industry (*Grupo Executivo da Indústria Automobilística*, or GEIA) created under Kubitschek's Presidency both concluded that foreign firms offered the only route to developing the industry. While anxious to enter Brazil's petroleum sector, multinational firms initially complained bitterly about the unrealistic idea of engaging in automobile production in Brazil, given the lack of "natural" conditions. Ford was particularly difficult, referring to the idea of automobile production in Brazil as "utopian" while claiming engines, as the most complex component in the automaking process, could not be produced in the tropics (Shapiro, 1994: 70). This was a similar claim that the same MNCs made about automobile production in India. However, these fears were put to rest as eleven firms opted to participate in Brazil's auto production plan, of which six were controlled by foreign capital, two were 50–50 joint ventures, and three were controlled by Brazilian capital. The industry achieved rapid success in terms of vehicle production, which reached 145,000 in 1961, as well as in local content, which averaged 90% in the 1960s. However, as Table 3 shows, the industry also experienced massive consolidation and, by 1968, was almost entirely controlled by foreign capital.

The contrast with India in the pattern of ownership of auto industry firms is glaring. The Brazilian state considered private firms incapable of meeting the technological and financial requirements of automobile production, a view that was deemed consistent with earlier experience in oil and steel. However, Brazilian firms were no differently endowed in terms of these capabilities than their Indian counterparts. If anything, Brazil was in a stronger financial position in the late 1950s than India, and the Brazilian government offered similar financial support to Brazilian firms as Indian firms received. The surprising difference was that, unlike their Indian counterparts, many Brazilian firms also seemed to share government's views toward the relative roles of domestic and foreign capital. It is especially puzzling given the structural similarities of the Brazilian and Indian private sectors in terms of size, organization, and sectoral distribution of the leading firms.

Further, in addition to having a core of large business groups, Brazil already had a relatively vibrant locally owned auto parts manufacturing sector that typically serves as an incubator for manufacturing capabilities. However, just as had occurred a decade before in the steel industry, Brazilian firms made it clear to the Vargas subcommission that they were unable to pursue such an undertaking, even if the state was to provide the financing (Shapiro, 1994: 43).

Table 3 Automobile industry investment patterns in Brazil

	Cruzeiro, millions	Ownership & control, 1956–60	Post–1960 developments
Willys Overland	30,819	Majority Brazilian Capital	Ford takes over in 1967
Ford	22,420	Majority Foreign Capital	–
General Motors	22,159	Majority Foreign Capital	–
Volkswagen	11,173	Majority Foreign Capital	–
Mercedes-Benz	8,888	50–50 Foreign-Domestic	–
Simca	6,454	50–50 Foreign-Domestic	Chrysler buys 92% stake in 1966
International Harvester	4,576	Majority Foreign Capital	–
FNM	3,224	Majority Brazilian Capital	Alfa Romeo takes over in 1967
Vemag	2,714	Majority Brazilian Capital	VW takes over in 1966
Toyota	1,548	Majority Foreign Capital	–
Scania Vabis	780	Majority Foreign Capital	–

Source: *Adapted from Shapiro (1994) Table 4.3 & A.2*

Meira did suggest state financing of an auto production company that could be passed on to Brazilian private capital, but minutes from two subcommission meetings on May 7, 1952, and August 27, 1952, reveal that parts producers made it clear that they did not wish to enter the industry (Shapiro, 1994: 64). Instead, they were content to carry out subordinate roles in the industry as suppliers and parts manufacturers, a sharp contrast to their Indian counterparts that were clamoring to enter autos as lead assemblers.

Even though Brazilian firms moved aggressively to capture new opportunities in both the pre–First World War and interwar periods, as illustrated by the rapid growth of new business groups (see Table 4), foreign firms captured the lion's share of opportunities that arose in postwar Brazil. New Brazilian firms struggled to gain a foothold in the postwar economy even with the dramatic economic growth of the 1950s and 1960s. In this period, the so-called *grupos*

Table 4 Foundation dates, Brazilian groups and subsidiaries of US multinational firms (%)

	Pre-WWI	1914–1929	1930–1945	Post-WWII	Total
Largest Brazilian groups	**64**	28	8	0	(25)
Largest foreign-owned groups	20	37	17	27	(30)
Subsidiaries of US MNCs	0	11	21	**68**	(131)

Source: *Evans (1979) Table 3.1*

multibilionarios were almost all foreign-owned, and "the development of the automobile industry was to foreign groups in the fifties what textiles and food products had been to local groups in the pre-World War I period" (Evans, 1979: 110). Three of the six foreign groups that entered Brazil in the fifties – Volkswagen, Mercedes, and Willys Overland – were involved in the production of cars, trucks, or buses (ibid.). Further, GM and Ford, which had been engaged in CKD (complete knocked down kit) assembly, sale, and distribution of cars since the 1920s, expanded into integrated local production.

It is worth noting that this dynamic was not limited to autos, as indicated in Table 5. Foreign firms also usurped local groups in seizing the lead in new and complex areas of manufacturing such as locomotives as well as in consumer goods such as radios and washing machines (ibid.). By contrast, these were areas where Indian firms were staking out ground. Tata Engineering and Locomotive Company (TELCO, which would later become Tata Motors) was the dominant player in locomotives after surviving battles with the colonial government over preferential treatment to British exporters, and other Indian groups were seeking to enter consumer electronics industries through majority partnership arrangements with foreign firms. The general pattern in India saw Indian business actors increasingly gaining control of formerly British firms, as Table 6 indicates. Indian representation in directorships would also increase and be reflected in managerial control as British disinvestment rose in the mid-1950s through 1960s, as seen in Table 7.

The willingness of Brazilian auto parts producers with experience in the industry to concede to foreign firms also stands in stark contrast to India, where the leading auto component firms were keen to partner with MNCs and

Table 5 Distribution of foreign and local capital by industry in Brazil, 1969 (estimates)

	% Foreign Controlled	% Locally Controlled	Importance (% value-added)	Growth (change in share of value added, 1950–68)	Technology Intensity**
Leather goods	37	63	0.6	46	43
Printing and publishing	0	100	3	71	86
Apparel and footwear	0	100	2.8	65	29
Wood products and Furniture	0	100	4.2	75	100
Paper products	12	88	2.7	129	114
Non-metallic minerals	21	79	5.8	78	171
Food and beverages	53	47	15.6	63	100
Textiles	29	71	10.1	50	43
Metal fabrication	38	62	11.4	154	100
Chemicals	76	24	12.1	187	471
Machinery	61	39	6	273	400
Electrical machinery	49	51	6.3	371	542
Tobacco	91	9	1.4	88	100
Rubber products	82	18	2	95	229
Pharmaceuticals	94	6	5.5	187*	1042
Transportation equipment (excl. auto parts) [i.e. assembly]	100	0	8.6	374	314
Transportation equipment (auto parts)	78	22	–	–	–

Source: *Adapted from Evans (1979) Table 3.2 & 3.3*

* Includes chemicals
** Based on scientists and engineers employed in R&D in US firms (NSF data)

Table 6 Shifting ownership and control of firms in India, by number of companies (1911–1951)

	1911	1931	1951
British	282	416	382
Indian	31	66	158
Mixed control	28	28	79

Source: *Kochanek, 1974*

Table 7 Shifting ownership and control of firms in India, by number of directors (1911–1951)

	1911	1931	1951
British	652	1,335	865
Indian	262	826	1,385
Mixed control	102	121	372

Source: *Kochanek, 1974*

become assemblers.[64] Indian firms viewed this as the logical next stage of growth, especially during this relatively early period when the worldwide auto industry was still largely national (it would not begin to truly globalize until the 1970s). Instead, the GEIA wanted to encourage a non-vertically integrated industry structure to leave the parts sector as "natural preserve for Brazilian capital," thereby legitimizing foreign firm dominance of the industry as auto assemblers and supply chain integrators. In further contrast to India, Brazilian firms didn't perceive foreign firms as nearly as much of a threat as their Indian counterparts, but rather as creating new investment opportunities. They interpreted similar material facts entirely differently, an outcome that runs directly against the predictions of structural-material theories. As the President himself argued in the communication circular *Relatorio*:

---

[64] By the mid-1950s, Brazil had a vibrant locally owned auto components sector and so was expected even by Brazilian officials to be potential entrants into the industry (Shapiro, 1994). The Brazilian auto sector had seen some development in the prewar period, and grew rapidly in the immediate postwar era. Though by 1944, there were only 38 registered auto parts companies, they produced over 2,000 different components. These firms suffered at the end of the war as orders were redirected to overseas-based foreign suppliers, and almost half went out of business. However, they organized and received some protection via the licensing scheme Advisory 288, which allowed the sector to recover strongly to 250 firms producing 8,000 parts in 1952, and 900 registered firms by 1955 facilitating domestic content levels of 30% for locally assembled vehicles.

Thus, an excellent opportunity would remain for national investors to operate, possibly on a more economical basis, specializing in the supply of parts and components to various or all aforementioned 'manufacturers' ... recognizing therefore the advantage in a horizontal industrial structure, from which emerges two types of producers: manufacturers, primarily foreign, and subcontractors, predominantly national.[65]

The difference between Indian and Brazilian firms' approach to foreign investment is further supported by evidence from US diplomatic cables from consular officials in Brazil. In the postwar period, it was common practice for US embassies and consulates to serve as intermediaries between US firms and local business communities. Embassy and consular officials played crucial roles in providing general information on the economic environment as well as specific information on local business and government actors as a means of identifying potential business partners for American companies. This is aptly reflected in a June 23, 1959 cable reporting on a Brazilian firm's interest in the manufacture of brake components for the auto sector. The firm contacted the American embassy to seek potential partners in the United States to provide capital participation and technical assistance. While Indian firms were consistently clear that foreign firms would be a minority partner in joint ventures, Brazilian firms appear much less concerned, with the American Consul General in São Paulo reporting that "Capital participation is primarily desired by the partners in the local firm [and] the [Brazilian] partners stated that the potential investor or investors may *assume the administrative direction* of the firm, *with or without the participation of all or some members* of the [existing Brazilian] firm."[66] By contrast, US consular cables describe how the Indian Amalgamations group, a Madras-based auto component manufacturer, was pushing the government to enter truck assembly in partnership with the US firm Studebaker, which by this time was having contractual difficulties with Birla's Hindustan Motors.[67] Indian firms strove to become manufacturers and assemblers, and had government backing to pursue this ambition, whereas in Brazil, the state gave little such support to local firms, a sharp contrast with India's approach as well as its own strategy in the oil industry.

Ultimately, rather than securing a lucrative subsector for local firms, Brazilian parts manufacturers were gradually edged out of the Brazilian market, just like Brazilian assemblers. As foreign assemblers entered the market, they

---

[65] Cited in Shapiro (1994: 55).
[66] Memo from American Consular General, São Paulo to State Department, June 23, 1959. US National Archives, RG59, 811.05132/6-2359, emphasis added.
[67] Archival documents suggest that Birla may have wanted to exit the Studebaker partnership in order to work with GM. For example, see US Department of State Instruction to US Embassy in New Delhi, October 15, 1957, US National Archives, RG59 811.05191/10-1557.

encouraged their overseas suppliers to follow suit, resulting in the Brazilian auto components industry that had been exclusively local before 1955 becoming increasingly dominated by foreign firms. A 1962 survey revealed that of 156 medium and large auto component firms, only 24 were foreign; however, these firms accounted for 52% of the capital stock in the sample. The takeover process began within the first few years of foreign firm entry, and followed a pattern that is typical in partnerships between local and multinational firms. For example, the Brazilian firm Albarus S.A. had been in the market since 1947 and began supplying transmission components to Ford in 1949. The company signed a technical assistance contract with the large American supplier, the Dana Corporation in 1955, which should have boosted the capabilities of Albarus and strengthened the firm. However, within two years, Dana controlled 63% of the company's shares. Dana employed a common acquisition strategy to gain a controlling interest, trading shares in Albarus for royalty payments and capital equipment imported under Instruction 113 (Shapiro, 1994: 202). Cash-strapped developing country firms face difficult choices in these situations: They can either refuse the new equipment, which facilitates an expansion of the business (and perhaps risk losing their partner in the process), or agree to expand while ceding ownership of their firm. This is a tactic that MNCs also tried to use in India, both during the postwar ISI period and especially during liberalization in the 1990s. However, they had significantly less success due to major policy interventions by the Indian government, driven by continued insistence by Indian business and government on retaining Indian control of industry. By contrast, the Brazilian government offered little protection to Brazilian firms, and by the mid-1960s, the auto components sector was dominated by multinationals.

The analysis of diplomatic cables reveals similarly contrasting preferences in the area of tractor manufacturing, a crucially important and potentially lucrative arena given the huge scale of commercial agriculture in Brazil. On November 16–20, 1959, the São Paulo State Secretariat of Agriculture sponsored a symposium on the Manufacture of Tractors and Agricultural Equipment that was well attended by senior representatives of key government agencies, including the GEIA, the Brazilian National Development Bank (BNDE), and the Bureau for Currency and Credit (SUMOC), as well as business figures and others. A key outcome of the initiative was the view that "The technical and administrative experience of the motor vehicle and parts industry should be put to good use, without prejudice, however, to foreign traditional tractor makers who may wish to establish themselves in Brazil." The symposium generated a set of eighteen recommendations, three of which are specifically worth noting as they directly pertain to the role of foreign capital:

1. The motor vehicle manufacturing industry should be financed and managed by private industry and not by Government-owned or financed companies.
2. Foreign companies can better finance, organize and operate the motor vehicle industry than purely local firms; those already operating in Brazil as assemblers of motor vehicles will be given preference over other foreign companies.
3. Local companies can most effectively contribute to the National Automotive Industry Plan as manufacturers of parts or as sub-contractors to foreign motor vehicle manufacturing companies.

Not only was there little encouragement for Brazilian firms to become tractor assemblers, but there was also an explicit assumption that local firms would at best occupy subordinate roles as component manufacturers or subcontractors to foreign firms.[68] Any "discrimination" would be directed toward foreign firms that had already set up in Brazil over others that may come in later, rather than toward Brazilian-owned firms. This was precisely the opposite view that prevailed in India.

Shapiro (1994) attempts to justify the GEIA position by suggesting that neither Ford nor GM "with whom the Brazilian authorities had the most experience" had licensed technology nor partnered with local firms elsewhere, adding, "It is important to note that, at the time, no other peripheral country had successfully built up a domestic industry on the basis of 'national champions'" (Shapiro 1994, 43,fn31). However, this was the same period when Indian government authorities and Indian firms were engaged in negotiations with Ford and GM, as well as Chrysler, Fiat, and several other multinational auto firms. Even though their bargaining positions were similar, as the extensive international business literature on bargaining with multinationals would hold (cf. Vernon, 1971; Encarnation and Wells, 1985; Kobrin, 1987), and they faced the same financial and technological constraints as their Brazilian counterparts, Indian business and state actors nevertheless had an entirely different approach to foreign investment.

Indian capital also explicitly recognized the differences in the Indian business *and* government approach relative to other developing country counterparts. In a January 1958 communique from the US Consulate in Bombay to the State Department, consular officials noted that while recognizing that Latin American countries were offering a range of inducements to foreign capital, nevertheless

---

[68] Memo from American Embassy, Rio de Janeiro to State Department, August 14, 1956. US National Archives, RG59, 823.3331/8-1456.

> ... the [Indian] business community is not prepared to go to the same lengths as its counterpart in Latin American countries in attracting foreign investment. The average Indian business prefers foreign investment which does not entail foreign overall control. There is also a tendency to suggest that the foreign private enterprise has a duty to invest in India and collaborate with Indian enterprise, not so much with a profit motive as with a view to helping Indian democracy and economy.[69]

The communique continued by quoting a reaction from one of India's leading business figures.

> Typical of such attitude is the following from Mr. R.D. Birla of the Birla house (one of the two largest Indian conglomerates): "While it is not possible for India, unfortunately, to offer the same facilities and concessions to foreign investors as is done in some of the Latin American countries, the need for foreign investments in this country at this juncture requires little emphasis ... We would, therefore, heartily welcome any American investments that might come forth and contribute to the success of the (Second Five Year) Plan, thereby strengthening the foundations of democracy in this country."[70]

These preferences resulted in different market outcomes even with the same US multinational firms that eventually dominated the Brazilian market. For example, General Motors had been present in India as a pure CKD assembler since 1928 but despite government pressure refused to take on an Indian partner in the postindependence period and shift to integrated production. As a result, the government gradually withdrew its license and GM was obliged to exit the market in the 1950s. The decision was highly discussed in foreign business and diplomatic circles in India. Indeed, GM's forced departure was often cited by US embassy officials and visiting American investors as an indication of the Indian government's dim attitude toward foreign firms that refused to progressively indigenize their manufacturing activities (rather than simply importing components made in their home country and piecing them together in India) or work with local partners such that they could strengthen their own manufacturing capabilities.

On the other hand, Ford agreed to partner with Mahindra and Mahindra and remained in the country. Chrysler similarly agreed to support Premier Motors' auto assembly efforts, as did Studebaker partner with Hindustan Motors. As already noted, these outcomes had important long-run effects on the development of Indian manufacturing capabilities in the sector. Mahindra and Mahindra

---

[69] Cable from US Consular Officials to the Secretary of State, US National Archives, RG59, 811.05191/3-2058. The cable notes that a *New York Times* piece had been circulated among leading Indian business figures to garner reactions.
[70] Ibid.

is now one of India's largest indigenously owned auto assemblers, and in interviews, firm officials consistently cited the manufacturing experience gained in the postindependence era as an important factor in their current success. The same holds for other leading Indian firms such as Tata Motors and Bajaj Auto. This speaks to the long-term implications of these radically different Indian and Brazilian FDI preferences in the postwar period for shaping the relationship between foreign and domestic firms and industry and market structure over the long term. It indicates significant differences in Brazilian and Indian perspectives on the role of national firms in the industrial development project.

Finally, the Brazilian government also eschewed the state ownership option, in contrast to its approach in oil, even though there was already a well-positioned state-owned automobile firm in place. The National Motor Factory (Fabricio Nacional de Motores, FNM) was established during the Second World War to manufacture airplane engines for the Allied war effort and, with the transition away from wartime production, provided an option for the Brazilian government's auto production plans. In fact, in 1948, well before the GEIA was convened, the firm was assembling trucks under technology license from the Italian company Isotta-Franschini, producing 50 trucks per year with 30% domestic content. Though Isotta went out of business in 1951, the Italian government arranged a new contract for a more technologically advanced truck with Alfa Romeo. By 1956, FNM was producing trucks with 70% domestic content and was credited with providing a large boost to the locally owned auto components industry. However, the government decided that its performance was weak and Meira's GEIA report hardly mentioned FNM. The final plan ultimately accorded the firm a marginal role in an industrial plan dominated by foreign capital, and consistent with the pattern outlined earlier, its foreign partner Alfa Romeo eventually bought out FNM. By contrast, while there was little state ownership in the Indian auto industry in its initial few decades (as compared to other areas of heavy industry such as chemicals and steel that were deemed to be at the "commanding heights"), in the early 1980s India launched a state-owned auto firm with minority participation by Suzuki that would become the centerpiece of a new approach to industrial policy. The joint venture Maruti Udyog received heavy financial support and policy protection and quickly dominated the passenger car segment. Even more importantly, Maruti revolutionized the Indian auto industry by introducing modern production technologies and, much like FNM, facilitated major capability upgrading among Indian auto component producers particularly through the introduction of Japanese production processes and techniques. Just as the aging Hindustan Motors Ambassador represented the protectionism of import substituting industrialization policies, the new Maruti-Suzuki 800 would symbolize the possibilities of the unfolding liberalization era.

8 Conclusion

This Element has analyzed striking variation in the ways that state actors in India and Brazil perceived the role of foreign firms in the industrial development project. It showed how, despite occupying similar structural positions in the emerging postwar global economic order and perceiving similar development challenges, policymakers in Brazil and India pursued radically different approaches to regulating foreign firms. This variation was driven by divergent historical experiences in each country's late colonial and early independence periods that produced contrasting beliefs about the developmental role of FDI. The implications of these distinct economic nationalisms are reflected in the divergent industrial policies that were employed in both countries in the oil and automobile industries. The analysis in this Element seeks to strengthen existing theories of economic nationalism by highlighting the role of social, historical, and political processes in shaping nationalist beliefs and policy outcomes.

A central part of the discussion has been on the relationship between multinational corporations and the state. As has been highlighted throughout the Element, the postwar years represented a moment when multinational capital, particularly from the United States, emerged as a key actor in the global economy. Yet, it is also important to stress that, despite the growing power of the multinational firm, states remained the central actors in determining whether foreign firms could gain entry to the markets of sovereign countries, and the conditions under which they would be allowed to operate in their territories. This was recognized by observers at the time, with even American consular officials concluding in internal state department discussion that "Instead of the Marxian picture of foreign capitalists who have saturated the investment market in their own country and await an opportunity to spread their tentacles to unexploited regions, the picture is one of diffident capital which definitely prefers the home country as its sphere and has to be encouraged and provided with greater assurances when it goes abroad."[71]

It is also important to note that policymakers recognized that some degree of foreign participation was necessary across the oil and automobile industries in Brazil and India, primarily for the technology that it was expected to bring as well

---

[71] Confidential memo from the American Consular General, Bombay, to the State Department, June 1, 1949. US National Archives, RG59, 811.503145/6-149. This view was shared following discussions between the managing directors of several major American companies including Caltex (petroleum), Firestone (rubber), General Motors (autos), and American Cynamid (chemicals) on their experiences in India and their views on investment prospects in the country.

as the hard currency inflows it could provide. Economic nationalism rarely means the total exclusion of foreign capital. Nevertheless, the regulatory approach to foreign investment across key industries in both countries was markedly different. Both pursued "nationalistic" policies, but the content and implications of Brazilian and Indian economic nationalisms were radically different. Ultimately, the FDI policy regime adopted in Brazilian autos emphasized domestic production by MNCs behind high tariff barriers as a means of reducing imports, with private domestic firms relegated to subordinate positions, while the rationale of Indian industry policy rested on promoting domestic rather than foreign ownership and control of firms in the technology-intensive manufacturing sector. By contrast, Brazilian policymakers severely restricted foreign participation in the oil industry, seeing the foreign oil "trusts" as neo-imperial instruments seeking to exploit Brazil's natural resource wealth. Indian policymakers also saw the oil majors as neo-imperial forces, yet still granted them significant concessions and allowed them to establish dominant positions in all aspects of the strategically crucial petroleum sector, from exploration to refining and distribution.

Further, the implications of these contrasting economic nationalisms are not only important for developing this crucial concept, they also had major implications for patterns of ownership and control in both industries that persist to this day. The Brazilian auto industry was launched with MNCs playing a dominant role, a position that was consolidated over the course of the first fifteen years such that the Brazilian auto industry is now dominated by foreign firms. By contrast, Indian firms carved out positions in their nascent auto industry, and while not all have survived, many such as Tata, Mahindra, and Bajaj built on these initial footholds throughout the import substitution period and remain important players through the contemporary era of economic liberalization.

Finally, in focusing on the role of economic nationalism in shaping FDI policy in Brazil and India, this Element has largely centered on the question of whether private domestic or foreign capital would be privileged by the state in the oil and auto industries. Of course, the state-owned company Petrobrás has been shown to be crucial in oil, much as the state-owned Maruti would be central to the transformation of the Indian auto sector in the late 1970s and 1980s in collaboration with the Japanese firm Suzuki. However, the foreign-domestic distinction is not the only important feature of corporate ownership and industry structure. A central question in the postwar period was the role of the state in the direct control of productive firms (cf. Musacchio and Lazzarini, 2014). Both the postwar Vargas and Nehruvian administrations are typically considered to be "statist" and, of course, state ownership of firms was a widely accepted practice throughout the postwar developing and industrialized world before the privatization waves that would later sweep the world with the rise of neoliberalism. Yet in developing the steel industries in both countries, the private firm Tata Steel would emerge as the most important entity in India while in Brazil the state-owned firm Companhia Siderúrgica Nacional (CSN) would dominate. What can be inferred from this difference in outcomes? This final section briefly considers the question of the extent to which economic nationalism may lead to state or private control, using steel – the prototypical nationalist industry – as an intermediate case.

To do so, it centers on a key distinction across the Indian and Brazilian steel industry cases: the extent to which domestic firms were believed to have the capacity to play a major role in the development of steel. It suggests that in Brazil, domestic firms were seen as unreliable by the state, leading to policies that enabled foreign capital participation, whereas in India, domestic capital was considered to be a viable option in developing a strong steel sector. However, this distinction was a more fundamental product of historical contingency, as is briefly shown next.

To be sure, this is not to say that there was no role for state ownership in India. On the contrary, so-called public sector units (PSUs) proliferated during the Nehru years and have retained central positions in the economy ever since, dominating key sectors such as coal and banking. Nevertheless, the question of domestic firm capacity was important in the decision of whether to rely on state or private ownership in the development of this key strategic sector. The most central factor, though, was these countries' contrasting experiences with foreign capital and imperial (and neo-imperial) powers (cf. Offner, 2019). Brazil experienced industrial planning with the United States as generally positive. Indian nationalists, by contrast, were influenced by the negative industrial planning experience with the British, from the promotion of "free trade" in the late nineteenth century to the tentativeness with which the British supported industrial planning efforts in the 1930s as power-sharing arrangements grew between the Crown and the Congress.

On the eve of the Second World War, Vargas decided that Brazil needed to have a national steel industry. There was significant concern with the reliance on the foreign-owned firm Belgo Mineira as well as on foreign imports. This concern was amplified as supplies of key inputs and final steel products were disrupted by the war. The Brazilian state failed to encourage private domestic firms to enter the industry. Instead, Vargas sought to engage with the multinational firms DuPont and US Steel. However, the military scuttled Vargas' plan due to nationalists concerns of the sort that have been highlighted in the oil industry case, and instead the state-owned firm CSN was formed in 1941. Nevertheless, the United States remained central in steel industry development efforts and was seen as playing a positive role. CSN involved extensive joint planning between Brazil and the United States, with key financing being provided by the Export-Import Bank. This was coupled with military cooperation with the Allies during the Second World War in ensuring steel supplies for the war effort.

The development of the Indian steel industry contrasts quite sharply with Brazil. At its core lies Indian economic nationalists' negative industrial planning experience with the British, which in part led the Indian Congress party to refuse to support the British war effort in the 1930s. In India, the private domestic firm Tata Steel had long been a nationalist symbol of Indian manufacturing prowess and the capacity of Indian industry. More than any other corporate entity in India, it epitomized the core nationalist view that India had deep manufacturing experience that predated the arrival of the British and so India only needed to throw off the yoke of colonialism to return to past manufacturing glory. Even more importantly, Tata Steel symbolized the ability of Indian capital to overcome colonial resistance and realize commercial success. The firm was launched in 1907 after a more than decade-long battle with the British colonial government as the Tatas agitated to begin steel production in India (Raianu, 2021). Despite recognition by the colonial authorities of the value of domestic steel production, not least to secure much-needed supply for its own efforts in railway and other forms of infrastructure development, the Raj nevertheless favored British firms and "free trade" over domestic options. Tata forged ahead, defying British efforts to subvert entrepreneurial effort by famously raising shares directly from the Indian public through an explicitly nationalist *swadeshi* appeal. Tata Steel would quickly show its value amid periods of shortages such as those caused by supply disruptions during the First World War. It would become an indispensable part of the industrial fabric in India in the postwar period and through the rest of the twentieth century.

Finally, the role of colonial experience in shaping contrasting economic nationalisms that this Element highlights provides a basis for deeper examination of the broader phenomenon of nationalism. Two such areas bear mentioning in concluding this piece. The first speaks to the current rise of ethnonationalism. Much of this has been discussed in the context of the Global North, in Europe and the United States, but parallels have also been noted in the Global South, not least in Brazil and India. There are many interrelated issues at hand such as the issue of "internal" and "external" others in the formulation of nationalist ideas and beliefs. These bring issues of race, caste, and religion to the fore, when considering how contemporary Brazilian nationalism has at times been mobilized against Black and Indigenous peoples as well as how Hindu nationalism is often explicitly oriented against Muslims.

Of course, it well recognized in nationalism studies that race and nationalism are not easily separated. However, somewhat curiously, the issue of race is typically ignored in scholarship on *economic* nationalism, despite the clear empirical role of race in the construction of economic nationalist beliefs. For example, the discussion in Section 5 showed how colonial authorities used race-based cultural tropes to claim that Indians were unsuited for technology and skill-intensive manufacturing activities due to their "inherent characteristics." These types of racialized characterizations were commonplace and were indiscriminately used against Indians, from laborers on the factory floor, to engineers and managers. Indeed, even leading Indian businessman GD Birla famously – and bitterly – recalled being forced to use Indian-only entryways for a meeting with his British managing agency partners. This Element argued that race-based claims were key element of British colonial efforts to delegitimize the prospects for industrialization in nineteenth-century India. And in response, Indian economic nationalism incorporated valorized histories of Indian industrial and scientific prowess relative to Europe prior to the industrial revolution. In this sense, even more recent literatures on economic nationalism may ironically reproduce the notion that the market is the space of materiality and rationality, where social constructs like race – and racism – simply don't fit, even while making the very constructivist claim that economic nationalism is a set of beliefs. These issues should be at the forefront of ongoing research in the field.

References

Abdelal, Rawi. 2001. *National Purpose in the World Economy*. Ithaca: Cornell University Press.

Abdelal, Rawi, Mark Blyth and Craig Parsons. 2010. *Constructing the International Political Economy*. Ithaca: Cornell University Press.

Acemoglu, Daron and James Robinson. 2005. *Economics Origins of Dictatorship and Democracy*. New York: Cambridge University Press.

Adler, Paul. 1987. *The Power of Ideology: the Quest for Technological Autonomy in Argentina and Brazil*. Berkeley: University of California Press.

Aitken, Brian and Ann E. Harrison. 1996. "Do Domestic Firms Benefit from Direct Foreign Investment?" *American Economic Review*, 89(3), pp. 605–618.

Aitken, Brian, Ann Harrison, and Robert E. Lipsey. 1996. "Wages and Foreign Ownership: A Comparative Study of Mexico, Venezuela, and the United States," *Journal of International Economics*, 40(3–4, May), pp. 345–371.

Alfaro, Laura and Andres Rodriguez-Clare. 2004. "Multinationals and Linkages: An empirical investigation," *Economia* 4(2, February), pp. 113–169.

Alt, James and Michael Gilligan. 1994. "The Political Economy of Trading States: Factor Specificity, Collective Action Problems, and Domestic Political Institutions," *Journal of Political Philosophy* 2(2), pp. 165–192.

Amsden, Alice. 2001. *The Rise of the Rest: Challenges to the West from Late Industrializing Countries*. New York: Oxford University Press.

Amsden, Alice. 2009. "Nationality of Ownership in Developing Countries: Who Should 'Crowd Out' Whom in Imperfect Markets?" in Giovanni Dosi, Mario Cimoli and Joseph Stiglitz (eds.) *Industrial Policy and Development: The Political Economy of Capabilities Accumulation*, Oxford: Oxford University Press.

Anderson, Benedict. 2006. *Imagined Communities: Reflections on the Origins and Spread of Nationalism*. New York: Verso.

Baer, Werner. 2008. *The Brazilian Economy: Growth and Development*. Sixth Edition Boulder: Lynne Rienner Publishers.

Barney, Jay. 1991. "Firm Resources and Sustained Competitive Advantage," *Journal of Management*, 17(1), pp. 99–120.

Bates, Robert. 1998. *Open-Economy Politics: The Political Economy of the World Coffee Trade*. Princeton: Princeton University Press.

Bayly, Christopher. 1983. *Rulers, Townsmen and Bazaars*. Oxford: Oxford University Press.

Becker, Gary. 1976. *The Economic Approach to Human Behavior*. Chicago: University of Chicago Press.

Beland, Daniel and Robert Cox. 2011. "Introduction: Ideas and Politics," in Daniel Beland and Robert Cox (eds.) *Ideas and Politics in Social Science Research*. New York: Oxford University Press.

Bhagwati, Jagdish. 1982. "Directly-Unproductive, Profit-Seeking (DUP) Activities," *Journal of Political Economy*, 90(5), pp. 988–1002.

Bhagwati, Jagdish and Padma Desai. 1970. *Planning for Industrialization: India's Trade Policies Since 1950*. Cambridge: Cambridge University Press.

Blyth, Mark. 2002. *Great Transformations: Economic Ideas and Institutional Change in the Twentieth Century*. New York: Cambridge University Press.

Blyth, Mark. 2003. "Structures Do Not Come with an Instruction Sheet: Interests, Ideas, and Progress in Political Science," *Perspectives on Politics*, 1(4, December), pp. 695–706.

Blyth, Mark. 2009. "An Approach to Comparative Analysis or a Subfield within a Subfield? Political Economy," in Mark Lichbach and Alan Zuckerman (eds.) *Rationality, Culture and Structure*. 2nd Edition. New York: Cambridge University Press.

Bonikowski, Bart. 2016. "Nationalism in Settled Times," *Annual Review of Sociology*, 42, pp. 427–449.

Buchanan, James and Gordon Tullock. 1962. *The Calculus of Consent: Logical Foundations of Constitutional Democracy*. Ann Arbor: University of Michigan Press.

Buchanan, James, Robert Tollison, and Gordon Tullock. 1980. *Toward a Theory of the Rent-Seeking Society*. College Station: Texas A&M Press.

Buckley, Peter. 2006. "Stephen Hymer: Three Phases, One Approach?" *International Business Review*, 15(2), pp. 140–147.

Buckley, Peter, Jeremy Clegg and Chengqi Wang. 2007. "Is the Relationship between Inward FDI and Spillover Effects Linear? An Empirical Examination of the Case of China," *Journal of International Business Studies*, 38(3, May), pp. 447–459.

Campbell, John. 1998. "Institutional Analysis and the Role of Ideas," *Theory and Society*, 27, pp. 377–409.

Campbell, John and Ove Pederson (eds.) 2001. *The Rise of Neoliberalism and Institutional Analysis*. Princeton: Princeton University Press.

Cardoso, Fernando and Enzo Faletto. 1979. *Dependency and Development in Latin America*. Berkeley: University of California Press.

Caves, Richard. 1974. "Multinational Firms, Competition, and Productivity in Host-Country Markets," *Economica*, 41(162), pp. 176–193.

Caves, Richard E. 1996. *Multinational Enterprise and Economic Analysis*. 2nd ed. New York: Cambridge University Press.

Chaudhry, Praveen K., Vijay L. Kelkar, and Vikash Yadav. 2004. "The Evolution of 'Homegrown Conditionality' in India: IMF Relations," *Journal of Development Studies* 40(6), pp. 59–81.

Chenery, Hollis, P. G. Clark and V. Cao Pinna. 1953. *The Structure and Growth of the Italian Economy*. Rome: U.S. Mutual Security Agency.

Chibber, Vivek. 2003. *Locked in Place: State-building and Late Industrialization in India*. Princeton: Princeton University Press.

Chibber, Vivek. 2005. "From Class Compromise to Class Accommodation: Labor's Incorporation into the Indian Political Economy," in Mary Katzenstein and Raka Ray (eds.) *Social Movements and Poverty in India*. Lanham: Rowman and Littlefield, pp. 32–61.

Dean, Warren. 1969. *The Industrialization of Sao Paulo, 1880–1945*. Austin: University of Texas Press.

Dinius, Oliver. 2011. *Brazil's Steel City: Developmentalism, Strategic Power, and Industrial Relations in Volta Redonda, 1941–1964*. Stanford: Stanford University Press.

Dobbin, Frank 1993. "The Social Construction of the Great Depression: Industrial Policy During the 1930s in the United States, Britain, and France," *Theory and Society* 22, pp. 1–56.

Dobbin, Frank. 1994. *Forging Industrial Policy*, Princeton: Princeton University Press.

Dobbin, Frank. 2004. "Chapter 1: The Sociological View of the Economy," in Frank Dobbin (ed.) *The New Economic Sociology: A Reader*. Princeton: Princeton University Press.

Dobbin, Frank and Dirk Zorn. 2005. "Corporate Malfeasance and the Myth of Shareholder Value," *Political Power and Social Theory*, 17, pp. 179–200.

Dutt, Romesh. 1901. *The Economic History of India Vol. 1*. Delhi: Publications Division, Ministry of Information and Broadcasting, Government of India, 1960.

Dutt, Romesh. 1903. *The Economic History of India Vol. 2*. Delhi: Publications Division, Ministry of Information and Broadcasting, Government of India, 1960.

Eden, Lorraine. 1991. "Bringing the Firm back in: Multinationals in IPE," *Millennium – Journal of International Studies*, 20(2), pp. 197–224.

Encarnation, Dennis. 1989. *Dislodging Multinationals: India's Strategy in Comparative Perspective*. Ithaca: Cornell University Press.

Encarnation, Dennis and Louis Wells 1985. "Sovereignty en Garde: Negotiating with Foreign Investors," *International Organization*, 39(1), pp. 47–78.

Evans, Peter. 1995. *Embedded Autonomy: States and Industrial Transformation*. Princeton: Princeton University Press.

Evans, Peter B. 1979. *Dependent Development: The Alliance of Multinational, State, and Local Capital in Brazil*. Princeton: Princeton University Press.

Fertik, 2014. "Packaging Industrialization and Selling It: State-Guaranteed Export Financing and Nationalist Industrialization, 1920–1940," Paper for the History Project "Institutions, Credit, and the State" Conference. Yale University. *Mimeo*.

Fagre, Nathan and Louis Wells. 1982. "Bargaining Power of Multinationals and Host Governments," *Journal of International Business*, 13(2), pp. 9–23.

Fligstein, Neil. 1990. *The Transformation of Corporate Control*. Cambridge: Harvard University Press.

Fligstein, Neil. 2008. "Social Skill and the Theory of Fields," *Sociological Theory*, 19(2), pp. 105–125.

Frankel, Francine. 2005. *India's Political Economy, 1947–2004: The Gradual Revolution*. Princeton: Princeton University Press.

Frieden, Jeffrey A. 1991. *Debt, Development and Democracy*. Princeton: Princeton University Press.

Frieden, Jeffrey A. 1994. "International Investment and Colonial Control: A New Interpretation," *International Organization*, 48(4), pp. 559–593.

Frieden, Jeffry A. 1999. "Actors and Preferences in International Relations," in David Lake and Robert Powell (eds.) *Strategic Choice in International Relations*, Princeton: Princeton University Press.

Frieden, Jeffry A. 2006. *Global Capitalism: Its Fall and Rise in the Twentieth Century*. W. W. Norton.

Frieden, Jeffry A., and DAVID A. Lake. 2005. "International Relations as a Social Science: Rigor and Relevance," *Annals, AAPSS*, 600, July 2005.

Frieden, Jeffry and Lisa Martin. 2002. "International Political Economy: The State of the Sub-Discipline," *The Political Economist* X 2, Winter), pp. 1-8.

Gallagher, Kevin. 2005. *Putting Development First: The Importance of Policy Space in the WTO and IFIs*. London: Zed Books/Palgrave Macmillan.

Getachew, Adom. 2019. *Worldmaking after Empire: The Rise and Fall of Self-Determination*. Princeton: Princeton University Press.

Gilpin, Robert. 1975. *US Power and the Multinational Corporation*, New York: Basic Books.

Gilpin, Robert. 1987. *The Political Economy of International Relations*. Princeton: Princeton University Press.

Gilpin, Robert. 2001. *Global Political Economy*. Princeton: Princeton University Press.

Go, Julian. 2011. *Patterns of Empire: The British and American Empires, 1688 to the Present*. Cambridge: Cambridge University Press.

Go, Julian. 2012. "For a Postcolonial Sociology," *Theory and Society*, January 2013, 42(1), pp. 25–55.

Goswami, Manu. 1998. "From Swadeshi to Swaraj: Nation, Economy, and Territory in colonial South Asia," *Comparative Studies in Society and History*, 40(4), pp. 609–636.

Goswami, Manu. 2002. "Rethinking the Modular Nation Form: Toward a Sociohistorical Conception of Nationalism," *Comparative Studies in Society and History*, 44(4), 770–799.

Goswami, Manu. 2004. *Producing India: From Colonial Economy to National Space*. Chicago: University of Chicago Press.

Gourevitch, Peter. 1986. *Politics in Hard Times: Comparative Responses to International Economic Crises*. Ithaca: Cornell University Press.

Greif, Avner. 2006. *Institutions and the Path to the Modern Economy: Lessons from Medieval Trade*. New York: Cambridge University Press.

Grossman, Gene and Elhanan Helpman. 1994. "Protection for Sale," *The American Economic Review*. 84(4, September), pp. 833–850.

Grossman, Gene and Elhanan Helpman. 2001. *Special Interest Politics*. Cambridge: MIT Press.

Gunder Frank, Andre. *The Development of Underdevelopment*. New York: Monthly Review Press.

Hall, Peter. 2005. "Preference Formation as a Process" in Ira Katznelson and Barry Weingast (eds.) *Preferences and Situations: Points of Intersection Between Historical and Rational Choice Institutionalism*, New York: Russell Sage Foundation, pp. 129–160.

Hall, Peter. 1993. "Policy Paradigms, Social Learning and the State," *Comparative Politics*, 25(3), pp. 275–296.

Hall, Peter. 2010. "Historical Institutionalism in Rationalist and Sociological Perspective," in James Mahoney and Kathleen Thelen (eds.) *Explaining Institutional Change: Ambiguity, Agency and Power*. New York: Cambridge University Press.

Hall, Peter and Rosemary Taylor, 1996. "Political Science and the Three New Institutionalisms," *Political Studies*, 44, pp. 936–957.

Hanley, Anne. 2005. *Native Capital: Financial Institutions and Economic Development in Sao Paulo, Brazil, 1850-1920*. Palo Alto: Stanford University Press.

Hanson, Gordon. 2001. "Should Countries Promote Foreign Direct Investment?" G24 Discussion Paper Series, No. 9, February 2001.

Hayek, Friedrich. 1937. "Economics and Knowledge," *Economica*, 4(13), pp. 33–54. (reprinted as Ch 2 of Hayek (1945) *Individualism and Economic Order*).

Hayek, Friedrich. 1945. "The Use of Knowledge in Society," *American Economic Review* 35(4), pp. 519–530.

Helleiner, Eric. 2002. "Economic Nationalism as a Challenge to Neoliberalism? Lessons from the 19th Century," *International Studies Quarterly*, 46(3), pp. 307–329.

Helleiner, Eric. 2021. *The Neo-Mercantilists: A Global Intellectual History*. Ithaca: Cornell University Press.

Helleiner, Eric and Andreas Pickel. 2005. *Economic Nationalism in a Globalizing World*. Ithaca: Cornell University Press.

Henisz, Witold. 2000. "The Institutional Environment for Multinational Investment," *Journal of Law, Economics & Organization*, 26(2), pp. 334–364.

Henisz, Witold, Bennet Zelner and Mauro Guillen. 2005. "The Worldwide Diffusion of Market Oriented Infrastructure Reform," *American Sociological Review*, 70, pp. 871–897.

Hirschman, Albert. O. 1958. *The Strategy of Economic Development*. New Haven: Yale University Press.

Hirschman, Albert. O. 1968. "The Political Economy of Import-Substituting Industrialization in Latin America," *The Quarterly Journal of Economics*, 82(1), pp. 1–32.

Hirschman, Albert. 1977. *The Passions and the Interests: Political Arguments for Capitalism before Its Triumph*. Princeton: Princeton University Press.

Hiscox, Michael. 2002. *International Trade and Political Conflict*, Princeton: Princeton University Press.

Hymer, Stephen. 1976. *The International Operations of National Firms: A Study of Direct Foreign Investment*, Cambridge: MIT Press.

Iverson, Torben. 2005. *Capitalism, Democracy and Welfare*. Cambridge: Cambridge University Press.

Immergut, Ellen. 1998. "The Theoretical Core of the New Institutionalism", *Politics and Society*, 26(1, March), pp. 5–34.

Jackson, Jason. 2025. *Traders, Speculators, and Captains of Industry: How Capitalist Legitimacy Shaped Foreign Investment Policy in India*. Harvard University Press.

Javorcik, Beata. 2004. "Does Foreign Direct Investment Increase the Productivity of Domestic Firms? In Search of Spillovers Through Backward Linkages," *American Economic Review*, 94(3), pp. 605–627.

Johnson, Harry G. 1965. "A Theoretical Model of Economic Nationalism in New and Developing States," *Political Science Quarterly*, 80(2), pp. 169–185.

Katznelson, Ira and Barry Weingast. 2005. "Intersection Between Historical and Rational Choice Institutionalism," in Ira Katznelson and Barry Weingast (eds.). *Preferences and Situations: Points of Intersection Between Historical and Rational Choice Institutionalism*. New York: Russell Sage Foundation.

Kaul, Hriday Nath. 1991. *K.D. Malaviya and the Evolution of India's Oil Policy*. New Delhi, India: Allied Publishers.

Keohane, Robert and Helen Milner. 1996. *Internationalization and Domestic Politics*. New York: Cambridge University Press.

Kindleberger, Charles. 2002. "Stephen Hymer and the Multinational Corporation," Contributions to Political Economy, 21, 5–7.

Kingstone, Peter. 1999. *Crafting Coalitions for Reform*. University Park : The Pennsylvania University Press.

Kobrin, Stephen. 1987. "Testing the Bargaining Hypothesis in the Manufacturing Sector in Developing Countries," *International Organization*, 41(4), pp. 609–638.

Kobrin, Stephen. 2009. "Sovereignty@Bay: Globalization, Multinational Enterprise and the International Political System," in Alan Rugman (ed.) *The Handbook of International Business*, New York: Oxford University Press, pp. 183–204.

Kohli, Atul. 2004. *State-Directed Development: Political Power and Industrialization in the Global Periphery*. New York: Cambridge University Press.

Krueger, A. 1974. "The Political Economy of the Rent-Seeking Society," *American Economic Review* 64(3), pp. 291–303.

Lake, David and Robert Powell (eds). 1999. *Strategic Choice in International Relations*. Princeton: Princeton University Press.

Lake, David. 2009. "TRIPs Across the Atlantic: Theory and Epistemology in IPE," *Review of International Political Economy*, 16(1), pp. 47–57.

Lewis, W. Arthur. 1954. "Economic Development with Unlimited Supplies of Labour," *The Manchester School*, 22(2), pp. 139–191.

List, Friedrich. 1841 (1904). *National System of Political Economy*. Longman Greens.

Ludden, David. 1992. "India's Development Regime" in Nicholas Dirks (ed.) *Colonialism and Culture*, Ann Arbor: University of Michigan Press, pp. 247–287.

Mahoney, James. 2000. "Path Dependence in Historical Sociology," *Theory and Society*, 29, pp. 507–548.

Mahoney, James and Kathleen Thelen. 2010. "A Gradual Theory of Institutional Change," in James Mahoney and Kathleen Thelen (eds.) *Explaining Institutional Change: Ambiguity, Agency, and Power*. Cambridge: Cambridge University Press.

Mares, Isabel. 2003. *The Politics of Social Risk: Business and Welfare State Development*. Cambridge: Cambridge University Press.

Markusen, James and Venables Anthony. 1999. "Foreign Direct Investment as a Catalyst for Industrial Development," *European Economic Review*, 43(2), pp. 335–356.

Martin, Cathy Jo. 1995. "Nature of Nurture: Sources of Firm Preferences for National Health Reform," *American Political Science Review*, 89(4), pp. 898–913.

Martin, Cathy Jo. 2006. "Consider the Source! Determinants of Corporate Preferences for Public Policy," in *Business and Government: Methods and Practice*. Leverkusen: Barbara Budrich Publishers.

Maxfield, Sylvia and Ben Ross Schneider (eds). 2007. *Business and the State in Developing Countries*, Ithaca: Cornell University Press.

Meyer, John, John Boli, George M. Thomas, Francisco O. Ramirez. 1997. "World Society and the Nation-State," *American Journal of Sociology*, 103(1, July), pp. 144–181.

Milner, Helen V. 1988. *Resisting Protectionism: Global Industries and the Politics of International Trade*. Princeton: Princeton University Press.

Milner, Helen. 1999. "The Political Economy of International Trade," *Annual Review of Political Science*, 2, 91–114.

Mitchell, Timothy. 2002. "Introduction" and Chapter One: "Can the Mosquito Speak?" in *Rule of Experts: Egypt, Techno-Politics, Modernity*. Berkeley: University of California Press.

Misra, Maria. 1999. *Business, Race and Politics in British India c. 1850-1960*. Oxford: Oxford University Press.

Moran, Theodore. 1971. *Multinational Corporations and the Politics of Dependence: Copper in Chile*. Princeton: Princeton University Press.

Mukherjee, Aditya. 2012. "Colonial Globalisation to Post Colonial Globalisation: Non-Alignment and South-South Cooperation," *Austral: Brazilian Journal of Strategy & International Relations*, 1(2), pp. 251–272.

Mukherjee, Aditya. 2002. *Imperialism, Nationalism, and the Making of the Indian Capitalist Class, 1920–1947*. Thousand Oaks: Sage Publications.

Musacchio, Aldo and Sergio Lazzarini. 2014. *Reinventing State Capitalism*. Cambridge: Harvard University Press.

Mylonas, Harris and Maya Tudor. 2023. *Varieties of Nationalism: Communities, Narratives, Identities*. Cambridge Elements, New York: Cambridge University Press.

North, Douglas. 2005. *Understanding the Process of Economic Change*. Princeton: Princeton University Press.

Offner, Amy. 2021. *Sorting Out the Mixed Economy: The Rise and Fall of Welfare and Developmental States in the Americas*. Princeton: Princeton University Press.

Olson, Mancur. 1965. *The Logic of Collective Action: Public Goods and the Theory of Groups*. Cambridge: Harvard University Press.

Ostrowski, Wojciech. 2023. "The Twilight of Resource Nationalism: From Cyclicality to Singularity?" *Resources Policy*, 83, June 2023.

Pandya, Sonal. 2004. "Specificity, Productivity and Tradeability: Toward a Theory of Individual FDI Preferences," Paper Presented at the Annual Meeting of the Political Science Association, September 2004.

Pandya, Sonal. 2014. Trading Spaces: Foreign Direct Investment Regulation, 1970–2000. Cambridge University Press.

Peltzman, S. 1976. "Toward a More General Theory of Regulation," *Journal of Law and Economics*, August, 19(2), pp. 211–240.

Perrow, Charles. 2002. *Organizing America: Wealth, Power, and the Origins of Corporate Capitalism*. Princeton: Princeton University Press.

Pickel, Andreas. 2022. *Handbook of Economic Nationalism*. Cheltenham: Edward Elgar Publishing.

Pinto, Pablo. 2003. "Tying Hands vs. Exchanging Hostages. Domestic Coalitions, Political Constraints and FDI." Prepared for the 2003 Annual Meeting of the American Political Science Association, Philadelphia, August 28–31, 2003.

Prakash, Gyan. 1999. *Another Reason: Science and the Imagination of Modern India*. Princeton: Princeton University Press.

Prebisch, Raúl. 1950. *The Economic Development of Latin America, and Its Principal Problems [by Pr. Paul Prebisch, October 1949]*. Lake Success: United Nations, Department of Economic Affairs.

Prebisch, Raúl 1959. "Commercial Policy in the Underdeveloped Countries," *American Economic Review*, 49(2), pp. 251–273.

Priest, Tyler. 2014. "'O Bilhete Premiado?' The Emergence of Brazil as An Oil Power," *Mimeo*.

Randall, Laura. 1993. *The Political Economy of Brazilian Oil*. Westport: Praeger.

Rodrik, Dani 1997. *Has Globalization Gone too Far?* Washington DC: Institute of International Economics.

Rodrik, Dani. 2008. "Why I don't do Political Economy Anymore" http://rodrik.typepad.com/dani_rodriks_weblog/2008/01/why-i-dont-do-p.html

Rogowski, Ronald. 1989. *Commerce and coalitions: how trade affects domestic political alignments*. Princeton: Princeton University Press.

Ross, Marc. 2009. "Culture and Identity in Comparative Political Analysis," in Marc Lichbach and Alan Zuckerman (eds.) *Comparative Politics: Rationality, Culture, and Structure*. Cambridge: Cambridge University Press, pp. 134–161.

Roy, Tirthankar. 2002. *The Economic History of India 1857-1947*. New Delhi: Oxford University Press.

Scheve, Kenneth F. and Matthew J. Slaughter. 2001. "What Determines Individual Trade-Policy Preferences?" *Journal of International Economics*, 54(2), p. 267.

Schneider, Ben Ross. 1991. *Politics Within the State: Elite Bureaucrats and Industrial Policy in Authoritarian Brazil*. Pittsburgh: University of Pittsburgh Press.

Schneider, Ben Ross. 2004. "Organizing Interests and Coalitions in the Politics of Market Reform in Latin America," *World Politics*, 56 (April), pp. 456–479.

Scott, James. 1998. *Seeing Like a State: How Certain Schemes to Improve the Human Condition Have Failed*. London: Yale University Press.

Scott, W. Richard. 2008. *Institutions and Organizations: Ideas and Interests*. Sage Publications.

Sewell, William. 1992. "A Theory of Structure: Duality, Agency and Transformation," *The American Journal of Sociology*, 98(1, July), pp. 1–29.

Shapiro, Helen. 1994. *Engines of Growth: The State and Transnational Auto Companies in Brazil*. Cambridge: Cambridge University Press.

Shulman, Stephen. 2000. "National Sources of International Economic Integration," *International Studies Quarterly*, 44(3, Sep), pp. 365–390.

Sikkink, Kathryn. 1991. *Ideas and Institutions: Developmentalism in Argentina and Brazil*. Ithaca: Cornell University Press.

Singer, Hans W. (May 1950) "The Distribution of Gains between Investing and Borrowing Countries," *American Economic Review, Papers and Proceedings*, XL(2), pp. 473–485.

Skidmore, Thomas. 1967. *Politics in Brazil, 1930–1964: An Experiment in Democracy*. Oxford: Oxford University Press.

Skidmore, Thomas. 1969. *Brazil: De Getúlio Vargas a Castelo Branco, 1930–1964*. São Paulo: Editôra Saga.

Skidmore, Thomas. 1988. *The Politics of Military Rule in Brazil, 1964–85*. Oxford: Oxford University Press.

Slater, Dan and May Tudor. 2021. "Nationalism, Authoritarianism, and Democracy: Historical Lessons from South and South-east Asia," *Perspectives on Politics*, 19(3), pp. 706–722.

Slobodian, Quinn. 2018. *Globalists: The End of Empire and the Birth of Neoliberalism*. Cambridge: Harvard University Press.

Smith, Peter Seaborn. 1976. *Oil and Politics in Modern Brazil*. Toronto: MacMillan of Canada.

Stigler, George. 1971. "The Theory of Economic Regulation," *Bell Journal of Economics and Management Science*, 2(Spring), pp. 3–21.

Stolper, Wolfgang F., and Paul A. Samuelson. 1941. "Protection and Real Wages," *The Review of Economic Studies*, 9(1), pp. 58–73.

Swenson, Peter. 1991. "Bringing Capital Back in: or, Social Democracy Reconsidered Employer Power, Cross-Class Alliances and Centralization of Industrial Relations in Denmark and Sweden," *World Politics*, 43(4, July), pp. 513–544.

Thacker, Strom. 2000. *Big Business, The State and Free Trade: Constructing Coalitions in Mexico*. Cambridge: Cambridge University Press.

Thelen, Kathleen. 1999. "Historical Institutionalism," *Annual Review of Political Science*, 2, pp. 369–404.

Thornier, Daniel. 1950. *Investment in Empire: British Railway and Steam Shipping Enterprise in India, 1825–1849*. Philadelphia: University of Pennsylvania Press.

Tirole, Jean. 1988. *The Theory of Industrial Organization*. Cambridge: MIT Press.

Time Magazine. 1949. "Brazil: Who's Oil?" October 31, 1949.

Topik, Steven. 1987. *Political Economy of the Brazilian State*. Austin TX: University of Texas Press.

Tyabji, Nasir. 2004. "Gaining Technical Know-How in an Unequal World," *Technology and Culture*, 45, pp. 331–349.

Vernon, Raymond. 1967. "International Investment and International Trade in the Product Cycle," *Quarterly Journal of Economics*, 80, pp. 190–207.

Vernon, Raymond. 1971. *Sovereignty at Bay: The Multinational Spread of U.S. Enterprises*, The Harvard multinational enterprise series. New York: Basic Books.

Vernon, Raymond. 1977. *Storm over the Multinationals: The Real Issues*. Cambridge: Harvard University Press.

Vernon, Raymond. 1981. "Sovereignty at Bay: Ten Years After," *International Organization*, 35(3), pp. 517–529.

Weber, Isabella. 2021. *How China Escaped Shock Therapy: The Market Reform Debate*. Abingdon, Oxon: Routledge.

Weber, Max. 1946. *From Max Weber: Essays in Sociology*. New York: Oxford University Press.

Wilkins, Mira. 1970. *The Emergence of Multinational Enterprise: American Business Abroad from the Colonial Era to 1914*. Cambridge: Harvard University Press.

Wilkins, Mira. 1974. *The Maturing of Multinational Enterprise: American Business Abroad from 1914 to 1970*. Cambridge: Harvard University Press.

Wirth, John. 1970. *The Politics of Brazilian Development, 1930-1954*. Stanford CA: Stanford University Press.

Woll, Cornelia. 2008. *Firm Interests: How Governments Shape Business Lobbying on Global Trade*. Ithaca: Cornell University Press.

Zachariah, Benjamin. 2005. *Developing India: An Intellectual and Social History, c.*

Zaheer, Srilata. 1995. "Overcoming the Liability of Foreignness," *Academy of Management Journal*, 38 (2), pp. 341–363.

Acknowledgments

This project emerged from one of the chapters in my doctoral dissertation, and so I would first like to thank my PhD committee members, Alice Amsden, Frank Dobbin, Ben Ross Schneider, and Phil Thompson. In particular, my many discussions with Ben about the Brazil comparison in a dissertation that otherwise focused on India, coupled with his unfailing encouragement, led me to deepen the historical analysis in the cross-country comparison and expand the scope of the industry-level analysis, which has ultimately resulted in this Element. I owe him a particular debt of gratitude.

Many other scholars provided input on this project as it developed into an Element. I would like to especially thank Nitsan Chorev, Diogo Coutinho, Mauro Guillen, Patrick Heller, Wit Henisz, Roger Horowitz, Roselyn Hsueh, Sonal Pandya, Simone Polillo, Alvaro Santos, Prerna Singh, Ashutosh Varshney, Vinicius Rodrigues Vieira, and Gabi-Kruks Wisner. Bart Bonikowski read an early version of the manuscript and offered detailed comments. Aldo Musacchio and Quinn Slobodian generously participated in a small manuscript workshop and provided feedback and suggestions that significantly improved the Element. Richa Vera Udayana provided excellent research assistance during the final revisions of the manuscript.

This Element is primarily based on archival research, and so I am grateful to the librarians and archivists at several locations that I visited. In particular, I thank the staff at the Nehru Memorial Library and Museum, the Institute for Studies in Industrial Development, the Confederation of Indian Industries, the British Library in London, the US National Archives in College Park, Maryland. Special thanks go to the librarians at MIT.

While this research is grounded in archival research, it is also deeply informed by travel and fieldwork in Brazil and India. I am deeply indebted to the dozens of individuals in business, government, and civil society who took the time to speak with me and share their views on the issues of industrial development and foreign investment.

None of the research would have been possible without financial support. I would like to acknowledge travel and research support from the Department of Urban Studies and Planning at MIT, the MIT International Science and Technologies Initiatives (MISTI) MIT-India Program, and the Institute for Global Law and Policy at the Harvard Law School. Funding to make this Element Open Access was generously provided by MIT Libraries.

Acknowledgments

I am fortunate to have had the opportunity to present this work in a number of venues where I received very generous comments. I would like to thank seminar, workshop, and conference audiences at the Getulio Vargas Foundation (FGV) São Paulo Law School, the University of Virginia, the University of California, Berkeley, the Watson Institute at Brown University, the Hagley Museum and Library, and at the annual meetings of the American Sociological Association, the American Political Science Association, the Business History Conference, the International Studies Association, and the Southern Political Science Association.

I would like to thank the Politics of Development series editors Rachel Riedl, Ben Ross Schneider, and Maya Sen. At Cambridge University Press, Julia Ford, Naveen Prasath, Sowmya Singaravelu, and their colleagues in the Cambridge Elements Editorial Office were brilliant in helping to guide the process along, from contract through submission, production, and ultimately publication.

This Element is dedicated to my partner Aziza Ahmed, with immense gratitude for all her encouragement and support.

Politics of Development

Rachel Beatty Riedl
Einaudi Center for International Studies and Cornell University

Rachel Beatty Riedl is the Director and John S. Knight Professor of the Einaudi Center for International Studies and Professor in the Government Department and School of Public Policy at Cornell University. Riedl is the author of the award-winning *Authoritarian Origins of Democratic Party Systems in Africa* (2014) and co-author of *From Pews to Politics: Religious Sermons and Political Participation in Africa* (with Gwyneth McClendon, 2019). She studies democracy and institutions, governance, authoritarian regime legacies, and religion and politics in Africa. She serves on the Editorial Committee of World Politics and the Editorial Board of African Affairs, Comparative Political Studies, Journal of Democracy, and Africa Spectrum. She is co-host of the podcast Ufahamu Africa.

Ben Ross Schneider
Massachusetts Institute of Technology

Ben Ross Schneider is Ford International Professor of Political Science at MIT and Director of the MIT-Brazil program. Prior to moving to MIT in 2008, he taught at Princeton University and Northwestern University. His books include *Business Politics and the State in 20th Century Latin America* (2004), *Hierarchical Capitalism in Latin America* (2013), *Designing Industrial Policy in Latin America: Business-Government Relations and the New Developmentalism* (2015), and *New Order and Progress: Democracy and Development in Brazil* (2016). He has also written on topics such as economic reform, democratization, education, labor markets, inequality, and business groups.

Maya Tudor
Oxford University

Maya Tudor is Professor of Politics and Public Policy, Blavatnik School of Government and Fellow, St. Hilda's College, at Oxford University. She researches democracy and nationalism in the developing world, with a focus on South Asia, and is the author of two books, Promise of Power and Varieties of Nationalism.

Advisory Board

Yuen Yuen Ang, *University of Michigan*
Catherine Boone, *London School of Economics*
Melani Cammett, *Harvard University* (former editor)
Stephan Haggard, *University of California, San Diego*
Prerna Singh, *Brown University*
Dan Slater, *University of Michigan*

About the Series

The Element series *Politics of Development* provides important contributions on both established and new topics on the politics and political economy of developing countries. A particular priority is to give increased visibility to a dynamic and growing body of social science research that examines the political and social determinants of economic development, as well as the effects of different development models on political and social outcomes.

Cambridge Elements

Politics of Development

Elements in the Series

Rethinking the Resource Curse
Benjamin Smith and David Waldner

Greed and Guns: Imperial Origins of the Developing World
Atul Kohli

Everyday Choices: The Role of Competing Authorities and Social Institutions in Politics and Development
Ellen M. Lust

Locked Out of Development: Insiders and Outsiders in Arab Capitalism
Steffen Hertog

Power and Conviction: The Political Economy of Missionary Work in Colonial-Era Africa
Frank-Borge Wietzke

Varieties of Nationalism: Communities, Narratives, Identities
Harris Mylonas and Maya Tudor

Criminal Politics and Botched Development in Contemporary Latin America
Andreas E. Feldmann and Juan Pablo Luna

A Chinese Bureaucracy for Innovation-Driven Development?
Alexandre De Podestá Gomes and Tobias ten Brink

Claim-Making in Comparative Perspective: Everyday Citizenship Practice and Its Consequences
Janice K. Gallagher, Gabrielle Kruks-Wisner, and Whitney K. Taylor

Shocks and Politics: Understanding Disaster Preparedness
Jennifer Bussell

The Undulating Capacity of the State: Autochthony and Infrastructure Development in African Cities
Ato Kwamena Onoma

Constructing Economic Nationalisms in Brazil and India
Jason Jackson

A full series listing is available at: www.cambridge.org/EPOD

For EU product safety concerns, contact us at Calle de José Abascal, 56–1°,
28003 Madrid, Spain or eugpsr@cambridge.org.

www.ingramcontent.com/pod-product-compliance
Lightning Source LLC
LaVergne TN
LVHW011848060526
838200LV00054B/4223